HERO'S JOURNEY: QUANTUM STYLE

Hero's Journey: Quantum Style

HOW QUANTUM HIGHER EDUCATION CAN TRANSFORM YOUR LIFE AND SAVE CIVILIZATION

Amit Goswami, PhD
&
Valentina R. Onisor, MD

LUMINARE PRESS

WWW.LUMINAREPRESS.COM

Hero's Journey: Quantum Style
How Quantum Higher Education Can Transform your Life and Save Civilization
Copyright © 2023 by Amit Goswami, PhD

Cover Design by Debabrata Dey Biswas
Printed in the United States of America

Luminare Press
442 Charnelton St.
Eugene, OR 97401
www.luminarepress.com

LCCN: 2023903996
ISBN: 979-8-88679-264-5

Table of Contents

PROLOGUE

What is Higher Education about?

Disciples were asking their Zen Master a question. "Master, you look like us, talk like us, eat like us, put your pants on one leg at a time like us, then what makes you a master? Why do they call you a master?

The Master said, "Because I can see the mighty oak tree in an acorn, the soaring eagle in an egg, and the wise sage in a baby, they call me a master."

The moral of the story is direct. Unless you can see possibilities in a student, how can you help her to grow beyond her natural endowments, the base level condition? In order to develop this capacity, you need to explore and embody the desired possibilities yourself.

What are the possibilities you need to cultivate the most, possibilities that transform? This question is addressed in a story in the Upanishads.

Twelve-year-old Shvetaketu was sent by his father Uddalaka to study under a guru. For twelve years he learned and then he came back to his father.

"Father, I have mastered the Vedas (the most veneered spiritual book for Hindus), the sastras, and the ritual performances," declared the youngster proudly hoping for a compliment.

The father did not cooperate. "Son, all good. But have you learned that knowing which everything else can be known?"

The son was puzzled. "I do not understand."

The father said. "Bring a fruit of that fig tree," said he pointing to a tree. The young man quickly found a fruit and brought it to his father.

"Now break it open," said the father. The young man complied and found seeds. "Break open a seed," ordered the father.

The son did that with some difficulty. "But there is nothing in it," he declared.

"My son, that no-thingness, only possibilities, is that knowing which you know everything about the future of the seed, the whole tree, got it? The same with reality. It is made of no-thingness, we call it Brahman, only possibilities."

In today's language, the Sanskrit word brahman is translated as consciousness. Quantum physics points us to this wisdom, Reality is consciousness and its possibilities to choose from.

What are those possibilities that change us, transforms our base-level human condition to one that is happier and intelligent. Some of the possibilities are objects that always stay separate from us; we can sense them, feel them, think about them, identify with them temporarily. But in essence, we the experiencer remain separate and qualitatively different from the objects of our experience.

There is a second part of the Shvetaketu story. The son wanted to know more. The father instructed him to pour some salt in a pitcher of water. "Leave that pitcher alone. We will continue the discourse tomorrow." With that he went to sleep.

The following morning, Uddalaka asked his son to bring the pitcher. He then demanded of his son, "Remove the salt from the water."

"I can't," said the son, "It has dissolved."

"Now taste the water," instructed the father.

The boy did so. "The water tastes very salty."

The father inquired. "Tell me my son, have we lost the salt?"

"No father. The salt has dissolved in the water. It is now part of the salty water."

"In a similar way, when you embody the essence of brahman in you, it becomes you. *Tat tvamasi.* You are that."

Okay. Admittedly, the metaphor the wise father used is not perfect in today's standard. Today, we can separate salt from salty water through distillation. But sans that you get the point.

Quantum science is elaborating the message further for us today.

The essence of consciousness—we call them archetypes, stuff like truth, love, beauty, justice, wholeness etc.—dissolves in us when we explore them to fruition. We embody them and transform just like water becoming salty.

Obviously, the spiritual wisdom traditions of the old and quantum science of today are telling us one and the same thing. True education is transformation embodying the archetypes.

For that, we first need to change our worldview from the one that has mesmerized our education based on the primacy of matter (matter is the ground of all being) to one that quantum physics is insisting on—consciousness is the ground of all being.

The second part of the transformative change consists of exploring and embodying the archetypes.

Together, the two parts constitute the mythical hero's journey, carried out in the quantum style using quantum principles that has made it accessible to virtually everyone motivated to undertake the journey. You are invited.

PART 1

Education and Worldview

Introduction: The Problem with Current Education is a Problem of People's Worldview

I (Amit) once attended a lecture on how best to give a lecture, how best to teach initiates about a new idea. The speaker said this: first give a quick intro on what you want to talk about; then elaborate, elaborate, and elaborate. Learning new concepts is a lot like forming new relationship; the student needs to encounter the concept or person in different contexts and garbs. "That needs elaboration," said the speaker. He added, "At the end, again briefly summarize all your elaborations in a few paragraphs." He then proceeded to illustrate what he advised. It worked! At least for me.

Since quantum education is a new kind of education that few people have any idea of, we decided to follow the advice above.

Educators talk about lots of problems with educating the kids in our schools today. In inner city schools in many countries, a teacher's main job is to maintain discipline, not teaching. There are problems with holding the students' attention; additionally, hyperactivity is virtually every student's problem. Public schools even in affluent areas suffer from teacher qualities due to the power of teachers' unions. Even private schools are not entirely immune.

Lower education understandably is designed to serve mainly young people's survival needs required by today's environment. Amazingly today, Higher education by and large has also become job training catering to basically survival needs, only more sophisticated. As an example, in both natural and social sciences, students in post-graduate studies work as apprentices in their advisors' research project.

And then the society's chaotic problems infect the classrooms too: lack of parental attention, drugs, even gun-violence have infested even middle schools.

Everybody agrees about one thing. Education was better just a few decades ago. What has changed? What are the causes for the degradation? Is the economy worse? Teachers' unions, teacher quality? Parental neglect? Not enough money? College faculty spending too much time on their research projects?

Then there is the other serious problem, especially in countries with high degree of economic affluence. This is the income gap that exists between people who receive just basic grade school training and those who receive college and university's higher education. The former can only perform routine, mechanical jobs—blue color (menial). The jobs of higher educated people are generally white color (desk-bound). The latter is paid better because they are specifically trained to enter professions—science, law, social sciences, humanities, etc.

The cost of higher education also goes up and up in affluent economies of the world. In the olden days, this cost was quite steady. The same thing can be said about the time it takes to educate for certain professions; time taken for a professional degree also goes up and up.

What keeps people increasingly at the lower education level is a simple cost-benefit analysis. Is it worth it to spend so much time and money for higher education? It is a fact, that nature of human professions goes on increasing in complexity so much that what students learn becomes useless by the time they are ready to enter a profession. If this is the case, is it worthwhile to spend so much time and money to get a job training which is not even enough to do the job?

As a character in the 1977 Oscar-winning movie *Annie Hall* lamented, "Everything our parents said was good is bad: sun, milk, red meat, college."

Worldview

Actually, the real cause of the deterioration of education goes deeper; it is a worldview problem; worldview is what has really changed in the last five or so decades. What is a worldview? The worldview is the lens that people in a society wear to evaluate their experiences.

Worldview of the teachers affect what they teach; worldview of the culture from which a school's governing board is elected if it is public school depends on the worldview of the people who elect them. Even the worldview of the students, young as they are, determines what they want to learn and how. Even for private schools, though the school board can impose a certain worldview, but even so teachers' and the students' worldviews do matter.

A few decades ago, the worldview was quite uniform in most societies. It was called modernism—both mind and matter were valued. Mind in this context means the arena of all internal experiences—self (I-thought), thoughts (of meaning), feelings (of vital energy movements), intuition (of archetypal values such as love and truth). Matter pertains to what people experience outside of them—houses, school buildings, townships, rivers, trees, stars, and all that. The humanities and the arts, even life and social sciences taught about various aspects of the mind, aspects of human life, mentation, and human values; science focused on matter. Both were regarded as important.

The truce was tentative and uncomfortable from the science side to no end. Science's success in explaining natural phenomena came from its two-pronged approach—both theoretical predictions and experimental verifications were necessary—before something was accepted as truth. Religions on the other hand made many unverified assumptions—God, heaven, and hell, moral values (for which the archetype is goodness with the duality of good and evil)—for example. Religions operated more on faith and dogma.

There was a compelling reason for the truce, however. What we call modern science was formulated by the great Isaac Newton in the seventeenth century as a bunch of laws for material objects. Since then, we have discovered many more laws, but the basic framework of science—handling the movement of material objects in space and time—remained unchanged until quite recently. Most scientists of the modernism era saw the limitation of Newton's approach and initially agreed that there was no alternative but to go along with the truce.

The truce did not last. What changed? First, scientists in the nineteenth century "successfully" applied Newton's approach to explain the evolution of life as documented by the fossil data following the lead of another great Charles Darwin. Thus began a confrontation with religions' stronghold on the matter of life. In the nineteen forties, in a similar fashion, behavioral psychology applied Newton's ideas to explain human behavior as well. Then in the following two decades scientists made such rapid progress in understanding life and mind that by the 1960's many were claiming that everything in the world, every phenomenon can be understood on the basis of movement of matter alone. Religion is humbug. There was no more need for a truce with religion. Henceforth, science within the primacy of matter we will call materialist science as opposed to what science has been before which we will call truth-seeking science that has now gone underground. The materialist dogmatic worldview is called scientific materialism.

One more thing. The modern concept of liberal education—defined as dogma-free education that liberates people from religious dogmas—goes back to the eighteenth century to the time when democracy and capitalism were also founded. From the beginning, the separation of church and state was deemed as important, and this "secularism" became a crucial aspect of liberal education. In this way, from the get-go liberal education was dominated more by science than by religion.

You should see it now. When science declared its worldview supremacy, the conceptual lens of both lower and higher education completely changed in a very short time. In the nineteen eighties, metaphysical values were purged from our worldview albeit everything-is-matter philosophy is not verified truth but itself is a dogma. As such, it compromised science's avowed search for truth. Soon, value education stopped entirely in public schools and higher academia, even in many private institutions of learning—the ones labelled liberal.

And simultaneously with all this came the computer and high-tech revolution and with it, video games and information technology, social media, and cell phones. This gave materialist science considerably more power.

How Education Became Job Training

Mind processes meaning; meaning is a subjective experiential concept. It has ambiguity; it depends on the context—physical, emotional, and most importantly, archetypal. In fact, our highest, loftiest, noblest thoughts of meaning come from the archetypes— via the experiences that we call intuition and insight. Insights need the practice of creativity that uses the creative process of discovery of new meaning.

If, however, meaning becomes fixed and in one-to-one corre-spondence with objects, then the subjectivity and ambiguity is gone. What is left is called information; information can be represented as computer symbols that computers can process via an algorith-mic step-by-step approach, in the same way as in rational thinking. The concept of information fits nicely with materialist science in which archetypal values have no place. With archetypes gone, it is not possible to generate new meaning except as a rehash of the old.

With the development of laptop computers and the Internet, information became part and parcel of the materialist worldview, and it began dominating not only the academia but also the media. The media came up with the slogan "medium is the message." Media pundits decide the meaning of news and what would be the message. That attitude fitted nicely with materialist scientists deciding what nature is and is not based on the worldview of scientific material-ism. Shortly, materialist science with the help of the media began building the information superhighway with information replacing meaning as what kids should learn to navigate in schools.

Information culture eliminates the pursuits of new meaning and the archetypal values from which they come. The professions were initially created with archetypal values in mind. Scientists explore truth, artists the archetype of beauty, religious clergy the archetype of goodness, lawyers and judges the archetype of justice, healers the archetype of wholeness. Most importantly, businesspeople explore the archetype of abundance and politi-cians the archetype of power. In this way, in the olden days, pro-fessional training was tantamount to archetypal training. Now that archetypes are banished from education, professions have become just jobs.

Face it, this is how education has become job training. Both at school level and in higher education. Additionally, matter is reductionistic: micro makes up macro. Complex things are more sophisticated than simple things. As a result, higher education purportedly dealing with the complexity of the professional world has become highly sophisticated. This also puts it out of reach of people not interested in intellectual sophistication. Another factor for the lower-higher education divide.

Is Education Purposive?

Is education purposive? Does it have purpose? In the olden days nobody would hesitate to answer in the affirmative: yes of course. Without education people remain ignorant. Ignorant of what? Of their potentialities. Education reveals these potentialities as well as enable people to live a better life by fulfilling these potentialities.

We human beings have a brain that is built to foster 1) me-centeredness; 2) negative emotions by virtue of having built-in negative emotional circuits; 3) pleasure attachment augmented through pleasure circuits. These tendencies define the base-level human condition for many people. The potentialities mentioned above bring meaning and purpose in our lives. The best meanings come from the archetypal values. They set the purpose. As we explore and embody the purposeful archetypes, our ignorance gives way to knowledge and wisdom to use the knowledge appropriately.

In scientific materialism, human beings exist, like animals, only for survival; our evolution proves it. Survival does not require new potentialities; no need for meaning, purpose, and all big-sounding things. People can live in the base-level condition.

Get real! Say the materialists. The big-sounding things are ideals. Human condition does not allow you to embody these ideas; thinking about them may feel good; but what's the use? It is a waste of time.

This is another more philosophical form of the debate that is going on for millennia—idealism versus realism. Idealists claim that the ideals—the archetypes—directly come to us from our basic being; they are not our mental projection or imagination. Materialists say, Show us this basic being. Religions of course call this basic being God. So, materialists demand, Show us God." But how can we show you God if you refuse to engage archetypes?" The debate goes on.

Worldview Polarization

But fifty to sixty percent of Americans believe in God and religious values and similar percentages hold for many other countries. Of course, secularism officially excluded religious worldview from public institutions of education but elsewhere the religions stroke back (with a lot of help from politicians) and now we have a culture war and worldview polarization between the materialist and the religious worldview in many countries and cultures.

Unfortunately, archetypal values have always been hard to follow for everyone because of the human condition dominated by me-centeredness, negative emotional circuits, and the pleasure circuits. Materialists say that the human condition is our destiny; it is built into our brain, some of it from genetic endowment or nature, some of it from environmental conditioning or nurture. Materialist worldview enjoys a considerable amount of support because it has rendered the arduous archetypal exploration unnecessary.

Well, not entirely. Materialists additionally say that the values are still necessary to pretend in order to maintain the veneer of a civilized society. Political correctness demands it.

So, this has become another aspect of the polarization. Religions sell the faith in values; with values gone they would have nothing to sell. So, they decry the materialists' idea of pretension. If negativity is our true nature, why not let it all hang out? In this way, many people of religion have become major supporters of racism, sexism, homophobia, and all that. And yet, they also hold on to their faith in values, at least as lip service. How confused is that?

So now with the confusion of worldview, everyone is taking advantage of value confusion including the people who believe in religions.

With values gone, truth has become relative, and the media including the Internet breed fake news in some form or other.

The combination of all this has been disastrous to education and it lower-higher chasm. There is now a social divide. People of religions do not support higher education because not only higher education demean values but also teaches people pretension. They prefer that their education stops at the grade school level in order to escape indoctrination in pretension. They would rather let it all hang out—racism, sexism and all that.

People who are materialism aficionado do not seem to mind pretend values. They try their best to oppose racism, sexism, and homophobia. But more often than not, this opposition too, is a pretense. With dogma guiding them, their liberalism is as confused as possible.

The result of all this is that everyone in modern society lives in a balloon or tent of one's own selection: the liberal tent of scientific materialism and rational thinking (information processing) of people who *pretend to be inclusive*; and the conservative tent of people of a confused religious worldview that is openly exclusive; in America they exclude the minorities, feminists, gender-confused people. In India, they exclude the people of other religions.

In summary: Human values come from Platonic archetypes—Truth, love, beauty, goodness, wholeness, justice, abundance, and power. Our highest meanings come from the exploration of these archetypes. With values gone, meaning has become trivialized too. Additionally, emphasis on information rather than meaning has led to an educational system where understanding and meaning processing has given way to information processing. With information processing, kids only process other people's meanings which they have to remember only for a short time to pass a test. Subsequently, if they need any of that, they can look it up on the Internet. But they have no idea how to evaluate the information. So, they depend on the particular social media of their tent to tell them what is what. In effect, this opens them to manipulation.

Worldview Polarization and the Teaching Profession

The double whammy of the worldview of scientific materialism with its pretend values and the resulting polarization has ben very hard on the teaching profession across the board—both lower and higher.

Traditionally, people come to teaching albeit low compensation because the profession itself is full of meaning and purpose. Teaching students meaning and purpose, inspiring and arousing their curiosity and passion to learn—these are greatly satisfying rewards that money cannot measure. Teaching students to learn to discriminate and resolve their value conflicts enable the teachers themselves to explore the archetype of wholeness.

Although liberal education has always been dominated by the materialist worldview, before the explicit polarization, there were always centrists who saddled the fence, used the best of both sides, materialism for conditioning, values for meaning and purpose. Now centrists are rare in positions of power, the people who set policy.

So now teachers are torn between two pressures—pressure from the liberal wing to conform more and more to an information-processing materialist educational system with no meaning and values and the pressure from the conservatives to teach values but with religious connotation.

Consider an example—prayer. Prayer is natural to human beings as natural as the spirit within us; in our weak moments it brings us strength. Materialists are negative on prayer because it is "spiritual." On the other hand, the conservatives insist on public religious prayer imposing the majority religion on everyone.

There are recent reports of mass exodus of teachers from their profession that may or may not be true. However, there is truth in what the Columbia University Teachers College director of doctoral studies Dick Roosevelt says:

"There is definitely a crisis of morale and confidence [among teachers]. The belief that one can do good work and do good for young people and have a rewarding, satisfying career in teaching has gone down the tube."

In higher education, teaching no more counts for career advancement or getting raises. Dominated by the science model (where people get research grants and they need to produce results and publish to continue their grants), publish or perish has become the mantra of all university professors.

The situation is so bad that even publication that does not conform to scientific materialism does not count. So, the mantra really is even more constraining: conform and publish or perish. I (Amit) have been there. I did research and published but they did not count because "they are on psychology or biology, not physics; and when they are on physics, they are based on idealism." Go figure.

The Elite: the Manipulators

We mentioned manipulations before, people are manipulated into either this camp or the other. Who are the manipulators? There are some people who escape the worldview confusion and value confusion and are focused on wealth and power. In other words, they are worldview neutral as well as value neutral. Additionally, they have some leadership qualities—charisma and communication. They are of two types—intellectual and street-smart. Their common characteristic is that they are able to manipulate people by taking advantage of their value-confusion.

In this way, elitism has come back through the backdoor in a supposedly democratic and capitalist society that was supposed to have eliminated elitism.

This should not be surprising to the quantum afficionado. I (Amit) previously wrote two books one on quantum capitalism (the book was named *Quantum Economics*) and one on quantum democracy (this one was named *Quantum Politics*). I was able to demonstrate in both of those books that the most disastrous effect of scientific materialism is to create elitism in society just as in a previous feudal time, religions were able to do. The common thing between scientific materialism and religion is that both are infected with dogma. To eliminate elitism from human societies, we have to find a dogma-free worldview.

The Way Out

Is there a way out? Of course! What we need is worldview integration. Can that happen given the great chasm between science and religion? It can and it will.

Science has changed radically from its Newtonian science of objects; science is having its greatest paradigm shift since the Copernican revolution. And like the last time when the worldview changed from religious/feudalism to modernism, this time, too, the worldview will change, is changing. From science and religion—both dogmatic and unable to see eye to eye—to one integrated worldview.

This new paradigm of science is called quantum science based on the ideas of quantum physics the chief one being this: objects are not determined objects destined to move in a determined way; instead, they are possibilities, unmanifest until a causal agency, our basic being—consciousness—manifests actuality via choice (from among the possible facets one actuality), an event physicists call collapse. In this way, the manifest world is created from the unmanifest. Spiritual wisdom traditions from which religions originated have been maintaining this dictum for millennia; now it gets scientific support. In this way, science and spirituality are integrated.

The initial ideas of quantum physics came in 1925-26. It took a long time to develop and verify all the ideas; but eventually verification of the crucial idea of nonlocality—signal-less communication—happened in 1982. Nonlocality is impossible in space and time where communication requires signals moving with a speed limit—the speed of light. It follows that the domain where the waves of possibility exist, and over which consciousness presides is outside space and time establishing that the materialist dogma—Reality has only one domain of space and time—is simply wrong.

Soon the meaning of quantum physics and quantum measurement became clear, and a new quantum science began to be built based on this consciousness-based new meaning of quantum physics. And now after three decades plus, we have a full-blown new paradigm of science and the worldview based on it—the quantum worldview.

Since consciousness is the foundational ground of all being, matter and nonmatter—mind, vitality, and archetypes—all are possibilities of consciousness to choose from giving us the experiences of sensing (matter), thinking (mental meaning), feeling (vital energies) and intuiting (archetypes). Realize: archetypes are aspects of consciousness coming from the extrasensory nonlocal experience of intuition.

Are archetypes real? If they can be experienced, explored, and embodied, they certainly are. Quantum science gives us a science of experience as well as of creative exploration and embodiment of the archetypes.

The implication of this quantum worldview integration on education—both lower and higher—is huge. We will elaborate on all the concepts introduced so far in future chapters.

Consciousness is the Ground of all Being

According to quantum science, three fundamental attributes define Consciousness — the attribute of an ontological causal being of Oneness, called sat *in Sanskrit, the attribute of manifestation in various states of awareness/experience (of subject-object polarity), called* chit *in Sanskrit (this includes the ordinary state of the ego) and its attribute for expansion that gives us happiness,* Ananda *in Sanskrit.*

The first attribute defines the metaphysics, the second gives us a science of experience, and the third suggests that quantum science is also a science of transformation to "higher" (expanded states) happier states of Consciousness and about how to manifest these higher states. Naturally quantum science also tells all about pathology (states of contraction) of the normal and subnormal states and about healing them.

There is a reason that I am giving you some Sanskrit words. In science, we always trace back an idea to its origin. The initial research on Consciousness millennia ago done in India gave us the same definition n of Consciousness and that research was the basis of the spiritual wisdom (Vedanta and Yoga) tradition of the Indian culture. Those researchers discovered all their findings via meditation practices and creative insights.

Science as we know it initially started in the sixteenth century with emphasis on the object pole of conscious awareness; nobody knew if the subject of experience—us—can be studied under science. When quantum physics was discovered in the early twentieth century, initially that, too, was formulated as a science of objects. But to interpret it, to understand its meaning, and to connect the mechanics to experimental data, a surprise happened. Consciousness entered physics. Yes, Consciousness with all three attributes as discovered and defined by the spiritual wisdom traditions is the ground of being on which quantum physics is based.

Quantum science is thus the integration of science and spirituality. Wisdom traditions and science of Consciousness are one and the same developing science with a seven-thousand-year-old lineage.

But quantum science is also much more. The science of objects, Newtonian science, has one other limitation. Objects respond only to cause; their movement is causal. But watch why you are motivated to do things. Because you have an agenda, right, a purpose? Quantum science, being rooted in Consciousness, injects purpose in science.

Caution. To repeat, what we call science today is not real science, it is science with a dogma. The dogma is materialism: everything is matter and epiphenomena of material interactions. In the mid-twentieth century, American pragmatism took over the idealism of a war-torn world, and the metaphysics of scientific materialism began its run. This dogma excludes our Consciousness as we experience it, excludes the bulk of our experiences. In materialist science we are supposed to be sensing and thinking machines.

In the same way, spiritual wisdom traditions degenerated into organized religions. However, religions also come with dogma. For example, Christianity comes with the dogma that all life was created 6000 years ago in one fell swoop by the creator called God. No evolution is ever acknowledged in spite of all the centuries-old discovery of fossil data. In this way, this dogma excludes the phenomenon of evolution. Hinduism comes with the dogma of Brahminism—the genes you are born with can make you superior or inferior.

Dogmatic systems of thought—materialist science and religions—are exclusive; they are valid only for part of our being, but not all, never all. On the other hand, we must not deny the success of materialist science in producing useful technology that has helped civilization. And who can deny that for a long time and to this day, religions are the upholders of ethical behavior in many human societies?

Quantum science is totally inclusive. It is entirely dogma-free. It separates the chaff of materialism from science (matter is everything); instead, it finds the rightful place for matter: inanimate matter gives us the hardware for living matter. Living software comes from additional organizing principles of Consciousness. The laws of both hardware (material laws of physics) and software (laws of living including mentation) come from Consciousness.

Reality Check

What about the realist challenge, show us the basic being. One of the archetypes is the self-archetype. When we explore it to fruition, it opens the door to the basic being and as we go through the door, we encounter the basic being. It is not strictly speaking an experience, the mystic Franklin Merrell-Wolff called it *imperience* after he had it, but many people of the spiritual wisdom traditions report having it.

You may say, like the skeptical scientist, but you are not showing this being to me! No, we are showing you that from time to time there develop human beings who have such imperiences. They carry the fragrance of their imperience. Buddha, Jesus, Lao Tzu, Socrates, they were such beings. More recently, there have been quite a few such people: Ramana Maharshi, Sri Aurobindo, Teilhard de Chardin, J. Krishnamurti, Anandamayi Ma, just to name a few.

Most importantly, the quantum worldview is dogma-free—it is okay to challenge all beliefs. You explore the archetype of truth directly via creativity to find out what is what. It is gaining traction because people are tired of the establishment—religious or scientific—telling them what to do. Since creativity is part and parcel of the quantum worldview, we can change as needed. We can elevate ourselves up from the gutter of the human base-level condition at least.

In the same vein, quantum science claims this. If you experience, explore, and embody, you too, can directly go into the state of imperience with Consciousness, the ground of being.

If you want to see an electron-one of the basic beings of matter, a scientist will show you some photographs. But of course, a photograph is not the electron either, it's a representation of the trajectory of the electron. Think of the people of spiritual embodiment the same way; the movement of Consciousness regularly leaves tracks in these people; that is their fragrance.

If you still object, But it takes so many years to go through such an exploration, don't. It takes a scientist years of training before she learns how to experiment with the elementary particles and how to theorize. Then only she can interpret the results of the complex experiments that reveal the elementary particles. Why should it be any different for the exploration of Consciousness?

Religious, Materialist, and Quantum Models of Education: A Comparison

Religious education, many people still go through it, is full of dogmas and it teaches exclusion on the basis of these dogmas.

The same thing is true of materialist education. Because of its exclusion of values from its basic ontology, it teaches us pretend-values, inauthenticity. It trains people for jobs. Following inauthentic pretend-values and training for jobs—low paying or high paying—do nothing about lifting people from the base-level condition.

Quantum science and worldview connects professions to the exploration of the archetypes. Quantum higher education consists of three aspects:

1. *Learning how to think.* Integrate all worldview confusion and settle into the quantum integrative worldview.

2. *Learning how to live.* Materialist education is job training, not life training. Head centered, only rational thinking is valued and that too, only for the exploration of outer material experiences. Religious education teaches archetypal values, but do not teach, not even emphasize, how to live values. Neither tradition emphasize the importance of feeling and intuitions or inner experiences. So, the recipients of either kind of education continue to live in the base level human condition.

Quantum education teaches balancing the inner and the outer and also creativity and conditioning. It emphasizes the explorations of archetypes necessary to improve the inner landscape, such as love, truth, abundance. The embodiment of archetypes is called soul-making in quantum science. Quantum worldview and education gives you the choice of either living in the base-level condition and or living with a soul.

3. Learning how to make living in congruence with thinking and living. This means professional training with creative exploration of the appropriate archetype(s) engaging first outer creativity and eventually inner creativity as well.

For the educationist, the central archetype is wholeness. However, exploring other archetypes (within the overall context of wholeness) may also be necessary.

One final point in passing. For grade school which is currently head-centered, major changes will entail 1) inclusion of all experiences, especially, feeling and intuiting; and 2) balanced use of both creativity and conditioning; and 3) taking account of child development.

We will elaborate on all this in future chapters as well.

CHAPTER 2

Further Elaboration of the Education Crisis and the Quantum Way-out

Before we begin to elaborate, I (Valentina) would like to share how I see what a book has to be like: a sandwich. A sandwich has two pieces of bread wrapping the "meat," right? The bread is easily digested; if you are hungry but cannot digest much, just eat the bread. It is better than nothing; you get some nourishment. However, the "meat" is all inside the wraps; it is all in the elaboration. Eat deep; it will nourish you to wisdom.

Human beings without education suffer from a base-level human condition that keeps them at a level quite close to machines and also close to their animal ancestry throughout their entire life. This has been recognized early on. Spelled out, the base-level condition consists of:

1. Me-centeredness

2. Tendency towards negative emotions—fear, violence, anger, competitiveness, domination etc.

3. Tendency for pleasure addiction

Human beings are social animals. Obviously, these tendencies are not good for building relationships and social consciousness. But what is proper education that can elevate us from these tendencies? Or is this question irrelevant? The answer depends on our worldview and especially how our worldview sees the nature of the human being and the purpose of education.

As mentioned earlier, currently, in the USA and many other countries, people live in two separate tents because they subscribe to two different worldviews. In one tent, the dominating worldview is based on religions—beliefs in God, moral values, non-material domains of reality; in the other tent, all-is-matter philosophy—a belief that all phenomena are material phenomena caused by material interactions in space and time—dominates.

The strong point of religions is that they have been founded and developed on the basis of experiential insights of great men and women; these people directly experienced a oneness—call it Spirit—that momentarily connected them to all human beings and all things overruling their me-centeredness; even today, many people have spiritual experiences of oneness in some degree or another.

Based on their experience, these wise people developed the concept of archetypes—the source of human values; exploring, experiencing, and embodying these values take us toward the Spirit leaving the base-level human condition behind, they taught. Religions still teach these archetypal values; but they have watered down their explorations into mere rituals that give the parishioners temporary high but do not transform them. Religious education today is like eating the bread part of a sandwich.

Over millennia, religions developed some weak points as well. Spiritual oneness was converted into simplistic picture of a powerful God as king of kings sitting on a thrown in heaven conceptualized as outer space doling out judgments on His subjects; the idea of experiential verification was gradually replaced by the concept of faith which for most people degenerated into a dogmatic belief system; the religious teachers themselves did not practice the human values let alone embody them; instead, they joined the power games of ruling elites.

Modern science was born as a rebellion against religious dogma and power play. Its strong point was the notion that all theoretical-conceptual ideas should be subjected to objective consensus experimental verification for which the technology was gradually becoming available. Its weak point was that by necessity, what developed is a science of objects, the stuff that we experience. We—the experiencers—was left out.

But a truce solved the problem momentarily. Science ruled over material phenomena; religions continued to have the authority to dictate over matters of human consciousness.

Liberal education which was founded in the eighteenth century along with the other two great institutions of modern times—democracy and capitalism—had from the get-go instituted a concept called secularism—separation of church and state. Unfortunately, secularism does not distinguish between spirituality and religion. In the attempt of banishing religion from education, secularism made it possible to throw away all that is connected with religion including what gives us human values to live by—the archetypes. Archetypes are stuff like love, goodness, beauty, justice, truth living which a human being has a chance of escaping his or her base-level condition; what insanity would banish stuff like that from an education curriculum? How can one engage in the arts without exploring the archetype of beauty? Or engage in science without dedication to the archetype of truth?

Both democracy and capitalism demand that the practitioners give up exclusive me-centeredness in favor of some other-centeredness as well; in other words, ethics is a must for both politicians and businesspeople. How can politicians and businesspeople engage in ethics without exploring the archetype of goodness?

How can healers heal without being taught about the archetype of wholeness? Without practicing wholeness, healers degenerate into curing their clients of disease like a car repairman fixes a car's problems.

How can people have meaningful relationship without engaging the archetype of love? Relationships based on just the pleasure bond do not last long.

By way of explanation of the insanity, let's consider a little bit of human history. In the eighteenth century, it was the turn of the

English to dominate the world and they did. They colonized India, America, parts of Africa, altogether about two-thirds of the world. Colonization was not something new. Previously, Romans did it, Chinese did that, even Indian and some other cultures did it too to a lesser extent.

Colonial rulers look at their subjects as inferior people; this is to be expected. And yet, the British colonies like India were large countries with huge population. To govern you have to use the locals to serve your purpose of governing. In this way, the British colonial rulers created the concept of education as job training. The idea is an elitist idea: if you want people to serve you well, you have to train them first.

Today, societies have developed elitism to such an extent once again that it behooves the elites to manipulate the lower echelon of their own society to serve their interest instead of personal interest. Converting professions into jobs—colonial style—nicely accomplishes that.

Fortunately, as mentioned above, in much of the past centuries, there was a truce between science and religion, and so liberal education did teach some human values within the constraints of secularism and job mentality and nothing drastic happened right away. Yet slowly but surely, the hard-core materialist faction of scientists took over science and by the decade of nineteen sixties, they came to declare the everything-is-matter dogma, a doctrine that eliminates all human values from the scientific worldview except as pretension.

If human values are not real but pretensions, then how can the professions be designed after them? In this way, the elitist power-play found support and in their turn the elitists began supporting scientific materialism.

After six decades of scientific materialism, the education scenario of USA and most countries has changed to something that only accentuates and perpetuates the base-level condition, not liberate one from it.

The Current System and Its Shortcomings

For children, under scientific materialism much of education is devoted to the development of a mental ego, beginning with learning the technical details of mental processing, the three R's—reading, writing, and arithmetic. Drilling the existing reservoir of meaning into the students' brain memory is then the focus of the various fields—literature, history, etc.—of the curriculum.

But this leaves out feelings and emotions entirely. How are students to be motivated to learn the three R's let alone process meaning, even other people's meaning? It takes curiosity, even some passion. These are emotions. The results show that due to this lack of emphasis on motivating emotions, many students go through the entire grade school and still do not learn to read and write properly, let alone do arithmetic.

Decades ago, after primary school, after the three R's are under some control, students were taught to ponder over the various subjects of the curriculum to learn abstract thinking—the meaning of other people's meaning. First in middle school, then with increasing complexity and degree of difficulty in high school, college, graduate school, all the way. This has changed.

I (Amit) still remember a lecture by Professor Alan Bloom in the late eighties when he mentioned this change. What is the purpose of reading old stuff, the so-called classics, except as information? The old meanings have lost their relevance; pondering over them is a waste. Instead, pick up the information; you don't even need to memorize the details, the Internet will do it for you if needed. In this way, you get to study a lot more books than ever before and really be knowledgeable. Knowledge is power. Knowledge is learning a recipe and how to apply it to get a job done. The more knowledge you have, the more sophistication, the more complex job you can handle. Naturally, your remuneration will also go up and up.

This is the model of education—education as job training—that creates the lower education-higher education divide. This also creates the elite—the few talented and gifted who escapes the regimen, learns processing their own meaning and even develop a sense of purpose.

Developmental psychology shows that at about age 15, the teenagers become interested in meaning-of-life questions: who am I, what is the meaning of my life? What is life's purpose? this sort of thing. A proper education needs to address these issues as preparation for higher education as well as continue on with the unfinished aspects of ego-development. But higher education a la scientific materialism has done a vanishing act. It is all job training now—lower education for low paying job, higher education for high paying more complex jobs.

Most human adults are acutely aware of the fact that they really care only of two things: 1) to have a satisfactory profession; and 2) to have a satisfactory love relationship. Scientific materialism fails in both accounts: profession as job satisfies the employers, not the job holder. You can use the money for pleasure; that only strengthen the pleasure bond with your job. But pleasure is not satisfaction! Likewise, relationships based on the pleasure bond provides momentary satisfaction when the couple engage in their mutual pleasurable activity, but what about other times?

I (Amit) once watched a TV show talking about relationships; their solution is to prolong mutual pleasuring to strengthen the pleasure bond. Their suggestion was that a couple should spend their entire spare time (evenings and weekends) in groping each other as preparation for sex, an act they agreed is difficult to spend too much time on. How practical is that?

Of course, educationists of the materialist ilk do not think that education should have anything to do with relationships. Quantum education in contrast emphasizes congruence between thinking, living, and livelihood. Quantum worldview flatly declares the importance of love in relationship; and love is an archetype.

Of necessity, we do have sex education as part of grade school education. Unfortunately, most teachers think sex education is about the birds and the bees, the mechanics of sex. Interesting. It is the religious view of sex that it is for reproduction, and that's it. Materialists push the idea that sex is for pleasure. So why hesitate to discuss the pleasure aspect of sex? And then of course, the question of how to make sex satisfactory in a long-committed relationship comes up given our brain's fickleness as far as the pleasure circuits are concerned.

Quantum science shows that there is another potentiality for the use of sex: for the exploration of love. Quantum worldview flatly insists that it is time to move towards this advance use of sex, sex for love, which then becomes love-making. Love brings long-term satisfaction in a conjugal relationship.

And in the same vein, quantum worldview insists that in order for occupations to be satisfactory, the professions must once again become exploration of the archetypes. In this way, creativity is guaranteed to enter our dealing with profession; creative exploration of archetypes brings new meaning into a professional's life, makes it dynamic.

When you engage with your profession as a job, sooner or later you will have a burn-out. Engaging with your profession in the quantum way makes your professional life dynamic, forever exciting, never lacking in satisfaction, and no burn-out happens.

Re-Visioning Education incorporating Quantum Science's Integration of Science and Spirituality

Our quantum vision is this: Higher education is education in human archetypal values that should elevate us beyond the base-level condition. This way—not being a job training—the current complexity of higher education would give way to simplicity and reduce time and money commitments required. Lower education likewise will not only teach the three R's but also three I's—Inspiration, Intention, and Intuition—and motivation will return.

Job training about the technicalities of a job should mostly be left to the job provider and the initiative of the person taking the job. Here concurrent changes will have to be made in the ways we run the economy, politics, and society in general; jobs must become professions again devoted to archetypes that bring on-the-job satisfaction to employees' lives.

All this should reduce the lower education higher education divide if not eliminate it completely. In any case, the society becomes civilized with the return of archetypes, meaning, and archetypal human values; no need for pretension. And people who choose to end their education with lower education will appreciate living in a civilized peaceful society and consuming the products of civilization.

Please note that people can change by consuming the products of archetypal explorations, too. A good example is yoga (stretching exercises) and pranayama (breathing exercise). Professionals should use yoga and pranayama because they are useful for creative archetypal explorations. Consumers do yoga to feel good. But if taught properly, you can feel good with an added benefit. Your organs slow down their activity anyway; this enables you to gain access to feelings in the body (see later), positive feelings. And then you can learn pranayama—breathing exercises—which will enable you to move vital energies in the body, giving you access to more happiness. The happiness comes from a momentary expansion of your consciousness, a taste of the happiness potentiality for soul-making.

Quantum science of development (see later) shows with proper parenting and teaching the quantum way, the scope for some soul-development is present in every child during the formative years. If in this way, you have the beginnings of a soul, later in your adult years you can easily develop a consumer strategy for soul maintenance.

You read good books, literature with meaning, to feed the mental part of your soul just as you use food for feeding your body. Trivial pursuit and informational reading are fast food, avoid that, at least balance it with meaningful reading.

Use yoga, pranayama, and Chi gong (the Chinese art of moving vital energy) for maintaining your emotional soul—your reservoir for positive emotions.

As Bob Dylan sang in the sixties, the answers my friend are blowing in the wind; they are in your potentialities. As you develop the quantum worldview using your potentialities—how to think— you will find that consuming the products of a quantum society will keep you happy in how you live. You have synchronized thinking and living at least. Two out of three is a pretty good bargain. And another Bob Dylan song will sing through you, "you don't need a weatherman to tell you which way the wind blows." You will know.

Re-Visioning Education and Social Change

Many educators have forgotten what the purpose of education is, lower and higher, what being a human is about, what the meaning and purpose is of human life and consciousness, of human values, of education, of higher education, of civilization.

To cut to the chase, this has happened because of the myopic ways we look at ourselves and the world today, our worldview. There is a worldview polarization to boot.

The word crisis is all over us. One crisis or another. Of all crises, the root crisis is education or rather the lack of it.

Decades ago, I (Amit) went to see a science fiction movie called *Planet of the apes*. I thought it was about extraterrestrials. Only toward the end I realized that the movie was depicting earth—our planet. And people were clapping in approval of the vision that we will regress to a planet of the apes in the future, everyone living in the base-level human condition entirely mindlessly, like apes.

There are many movies today that similarly declare that computing machines will take over our planet! Computer scientists theorize about how we could be better humans by inter-phasing with computing machines. And many people cheer that too and openly promote it.

The reason is not hard to find. In our me-centeredness human beings are like machines. We have some commonalities with apes, too; in our identification with the negative-emotional and pleasure circuits of the brain, we are like apes.

What masquerades as science today is a science of matter and mechanical machines made of matter. Materialist scientists apply their mechanistic science to us humans with some success; in particular, they have made considerable hay way in understanding the base-level human condition, our points of similarity to machines and apes. So much so that they are now openly saying something truly disastrous and untrue; they are saying we are doomed to our base-level human condition because there is nothing else; being civilized is nothing but being pretentious, being politically correct to create an appearance.

In this environment, and in the face of the perpetual environmental challenges that human beings have to face, the meaning and purpose questions, questions of feelings and emotions such as curiosity that motivate us toward higher education have receded to the background—producing the vanishing act I mentioned above.

Fortunately, to repeat once again, there is an end in sight, a new paradigm of science, quantum science, and with it a new integrated worldview. It is a science of Consciousness; it is a human science to begin with.

This new consciousness-based science is a science of all of our experiences including intuition that gives us glimpses of human values and creative insights that enables us to re-vision ourselves and our social systems—education, economics, and politics. With more meaning and sense of purpose than any previous worldview ever had, this new integrative worldview holds great promise in lifting us from the limiting base-level existence. Of course, a substantial number of us need to look through the lens of this new worldview and change how we think, how we live, and how we make our living before societal change can come.

Let's focus on education. Materialist education centers on the mental /rational with the assumption that mind is an epiphenomenon of the brain. In this way, currently education beginning with grade school, is mental education. But of course, children especially but even adults need feelings and emotions to be motivated (for which the emotions of curiosity and passion are essential); they also need emotions to make memory of what they learn since neuroscience has revealed that emotional memory is much easier to recall than purely mental memory.

Materialists think that emotions are brain's response to suitable sensory objects; for example, the sight of a tiger raising the emotion of fear. Could curiosity be like that? children looking at a star and responding with curiosity to know why that star twinkles and burns bright. But we also have to face the fact that such instances of curiosity do not last long.

The fact is this! Neuroscientists have discovered thar too much information processing reduces our access to brain's ACC (Anterior Cingulate Cortex) where the positive emotions circuitry are recorded.

For adults, we have another model to make up for curiosity: searching for money, name, and fame. But for children? Here is where archetypes become important. Quantum science shows that children's consciousness is highly conducive to archetypal experiences of intuition. They can get inspired very easily by nature, by parents, by teachers. The inspirations suitably guided give children lasting curiosity to make intensions to know.

Who Is Afraid of the Quantum Lens?

The word *quantum* was originally meant to denote an elementary particle—the building block—of energy. Quantum physics was originally conceived as the physics of elementary particles of energy and matter, but its message is radical. These elementary objects are, in suchness, not particles at all; they are waves of possibility in an unmanifest domain of reality for consciousness to choose from. As mentioned in the last chapter, there is now experimental verification of this unmanifest domain as the domain where nonlocality and instant communication prevails; this data contradicts the dictum of one domain of space-time reality of materialist science.

Out of fear of losing control, scientists of materialism are fighting back with equivocations. Maybe elementary quantum objects of the microcosm are exceptions to its rule, but who can deny the validity of materialist science and Newtonian physics at the macrolevel of reality where we live?

The founders of Quantum physics from the beginning had recognized the need for a correspondence principle: in the domain of the macro, quantum physics must morph smoothly into Newtonian physics. This was easy to demonstrate. Indeed, for an object in bulk with a large mass, the quantum possibility waves of the center of mass of an extended object become extremely sluggish.

Let's talk about the brain. Can telepathy between two people be explained by the two brain's expanding in possibility as waves and overlapping? In the nineties, I talked to a philosopher/writer whose model for telepathy was exactly that. But of course, direct calculations show that for two massive brains to expand and comingle, it would take more than the lifetime of the universe.

Does quantum physics apply to us then? To our brain? Can the brain's internal state of movement of all the parts around the center of mass be represented by a macroscopic superposition of possibilities from which consciousness can choose? Materialist scientists have made another seemingly good argument against an affirmative answer to this question: decoherence. Quantum possibilities waves of the different parts have to be coherent with one another, move in phase like dancers in a chorus line (fig.1), so that their totality becomes one macroscopic coherent superposition of possibilities. But at room temperature, the different parts cannot move coherently; instead, they decohere, the parts dance as in rock n' roll (fig. 2).

The question is thus indeed poignant, Does quantum physics apply to us, creatures of the macro level? But in truth, questions like these are put up to deflect our attention from the failure of the materialist paradigm in the microworld which already nullifies scientific materialism. The best defense is outright offence; so, materialists fight the worldview change by asserting that quantum physics cannot possibly apply to the human brain. Meanwhile all this kind of concerns have been satisfactorily addressed, books have been published (read especially our book *The Quantum Brain*), an entire graduate program now exist on the basis of this new worldview. And finally, most telling of all, definitive experimental data now exists, have existed for a decade at least, in support of this new paradigm of quantum science and the quantum worldview.

Figure 1. Dancing in phase (coherence)
Figure 2. Dancing out of phase (no coherence)

In summary: Yes, quantum physics applies to us. No need to be afraid of the fearful deniers. For the sake of completeness, we will present the theory now (see below); the supporting data is given in chapter 4.

We live in such myopia. Establishment scientists go on pretending that we are machines, we are robots with experiences that are purely ornamental; the experiences make us feel real but truly have no causal power.

Even the word Consciousness today creates consternation. What is it? Even scientists and philosophers of different ilk than scientific materialism have different answers that beg this basic question: Are we machines or do our Consciousness and conscious awareness mean something, have causal power?

A definitive answer—based on both quantum-based theory and neuroscience's experimental findings—is this: yes, consciousness, not matter, is the ground of all being, and yes, it has the most essential causal power of all: create the manifest world from unmanifest quantum possibilities. We likewise have the causal power of creating our own reality if we learn (education again) how to be in synchrony with the purposive movements of consciousness.

If you have watched the 2004 movie *What the Bleep Do We Know*, then the ideas above that we are positing are already familiar to you.

However, fear is contagious and some damage has been done. In politics, in America, as mentioned earlier, the democrats and Republicans live in different tents—a metaphor for saying that they look at the events with two different lenses. Democrats have bought into the philosophy of scientific materialism—lock, stock, and barrel. Republicans unfortunately do not do much better and embrace the religious worldview and end up opposing all science, even truth-seeking science.

The same situation prevails in the science of psychology. People of the materialist tent—the cognitive-behavioral scientists believe and propagate the machine view; people of the Consciousness tent—the phenomenologists, psychoanalysts, and transpersonal psychologists believe in the causal efficacy of Consciousness and conscious experiences.

Materialists, in conjunction with business elites, however, have taken over the practice of economics endangering the successful paradigm of capitalism. Sure, capitalism has flaws and it is incomplete; but materialism makes the flaws and incompleteness worse.

The field of education likewise is dominated by people of materialist tent—by people of the entrenched dogma of materialism—everything is matter philosophy—and they resist change.

People are confused. The mechanization of education and the prevalent materialist high tech culture, working in tandem, are dumbing down young people. Media talks about it, students are craved for meaning and purpose in their lives and do protest, but in the absence of any expertise in quantum science, they simply roam around from workshop to workshop by new age "intellectuals with Values"—a term created by the great philosopher-linguist Noam Chomsky—who profess new ideas but do not really challenge the materialist dogma, so do nothing much for the needed re-vision of education to remove your worldview confusion.

So, in this book, using the quantum worldview, we will clarify the basic questions of Consciousness which are also the basic questions of education. In a way, asking *What is Consciousness is* education, the beginning and the end.

How the Brain Becomes Quantum

Von Neuman discovered the observer effect: there is no quantum measurement unless an observer is there to look at the quantum object and its so-called measurement apparatus which actually cannot measure but does amplify the signal. The measurement apparatus, a photographic film for example, becomes a superposition of the same possibilities of position of the electron that it is amplifying. But of course, measurement does happen when the observer looks at the film since the electron shows up only in one position.

Von Neuman also proved mathematically that no material interaction can collapse a possibility wave of many positions into a particle of one unique position; we need a nonmaterial agency. He identified this nonmaterial agency as the observer's consciousness.

Von Neuman's original theory got bogged down with paradoxes, but I (Amit) solved all paradoxes with the help of the new metaphysics: consciousness is the ground of all being; all observers originate from the same Oneness consciousness. I even demonstrated how in the process of measurement consciousness identifies with the brain.

However, this theory does presuppose that the brain is quantum. can it be? Yes. We are forgetting something, we have been blinded by materialist thinking. Brain cannot act alone without the mind, a nonmaterial independent quantum mind; in perception, brain makes electrical images of the object to which the mind has to give a superposition of possible meanings from which consciousness chooses. See the brain's role as the role of the photographic film in the discussion above; it becomes quantum whenever it couples (correlates) with the mind; that is in the unconscious. It is the brain-mind which is quantum. With collapse, the brain and mind does become momentarily decoupled.

When the mind becomes conditioned, when it loses the creative quantum ambiguity, and becomes restricted within a small spectrum of choices in its meaning-giving capacity, the quantum brain-mind becomes more like a Newtonian brain-mind.

Rational thinking promotes the Newtonian brain mind. It has its place to be sure in education, but it must not be used exclusively. Especially when we are in the learning mode. In this way, the job of education must extend beyond information processing, must extend beyond rational thinking within a small pool of conditioned quantum possibilities. Education must make room for creativity for dynamic functioning of the brain-mind.

What is Higher Education Really?

What does higher education mean to you? Most people today assume that it is the education one gets in colleges and universities beyond grade school education. Most everyone also assumes that *higher* education entitles one to get a *higher* paying job. Sometimes one is actually able to land a high paying job. At other times, people discover that there is no availability of higher paying jobs that they are trained for and that they are overqualified for a lower paying one! The disappointment can precipitate a personal crisis.

Is that the crisis of education we were referring to earlier, a crisis in higher paying job opportunities for enterprising young people of the middle class? A situation that exacerbates the income disparity between the more affluent and the less affluent and shrinks the middle class. A situation of historically proven volatility.

Yes, but only in part. This crisis is part of a much bigger crisis—a crisis of civilization itself.

What is civilization? Today, materialists push the idea that technological sophistication especially in information technology and to a lesser degree economic affluence define the progress in civilization.

Fortunately, these attempts of misinformation have not been entirely successful; many people would still agree that civilization consists in our ability to live certain values, values that we call human values: truth, love, goodness, justice, wholeness, etc. Exploring these values brings *higher* meaning in our lives. Embodying these values makes our relationships exciting and fulfilling; we develop a sense of identity with our community in addition to our individual "me," a necessity for the successful implementation of democracy and capitalism.

Since the dawn of civilization, we have also recognized that we have certain built-in tendencies, this is what we call the previously mentioned base-level human condition on which we now further elaborate:

1. Me-centeredness: while engaging in any action, we tend to ask, *What's in it for me?* This transactional tendency we also recognize as selfishness.

2. Negative emotion: we are particularly prone to react to certain stimuli with negative emotions such as fear, anger, violence, jealousy, lust, domination, competitiveness, etc.

3. Pleasure-seeking: we have a tendency to engage in certain activities such as eating and having sex that bring us pleasure to excess.

4. Inertia of ignorance, we have a tendency to maintain status quo, for not to engage with anything new, including new meaning. This is the tendency that high tech materialists use to propagate an information-dominated culture. Information is thought processing without invoking new meaning, without invoking the facility of understanding.

Given these tendencies, how did human beings attain civilization even to the degree we see today? Historically, we know this. There were people in the past who not only overcame these base-level condition for themselves but also created systems of education to lift people up from their base-level condition. How did they do it? Via receiving knowledge from an extra-sensory source via the experience we call intuition that led to knowledge about how things really are. In this way, in these traditions, *education is purposive; its purpose is regarded as the removal of ignorance via intuitive knowledge.*

So far so good; everybody except strict materialists can agree. *But how do we get intuitive knowledge; what does extrasensory mean?*

The illumined people said, extrasensory means without using the five senses, direct messaging from Consciousness. Quantum science has discovered how such direct messaging takes place through nonlocal communication.

Can there be purpose? Has not materialist science long got rid of the idea of purpose? Isn't it only cause that can makes changes? Quantum physics shows that causes only affect waves of possibilities. Consciousness chooses actuality from these possibilities; it can and does choose with purpose.

The illumined people also said this: We are spiritual beings in addition to our me-centeredness. In fact, all of us come from

Consciousness that is the ground of all being, a Oneness. This Oneness has attributes—virtues that we value, these are what we formally call archetypes. Because we are *that*—Consciousness in Oneness, we can intuit these virtues when we fall into that deep (or high) state of Consciousness. Meditate, they said. It is hard work, but you can do it. You can discover the virtues for yourself. Explore, discover, embody the virtues. This is the purpose of the human life.

The disciples of the illuminati said, have mercy. Teach us. Tell us about the virtues. If we know what they are about, education will be easier for us; it will be accessible to the masses.

So, the virtues were codified a little and the codification continues even today. The philosopher *Plato coined the word archetype. We will now name all nine of them—as empirically revealed if you look at the major human professions even today: abundance, power, beauty, love, goodness, truth, justice, wholeness, and self.*

Higher Education-Lower Education Divide in Old Traditions

Millennia ago, in India, higher education *was* regarded as removal of the darkness of ignorance with the light of knowledge of the archetypes. The higher education so practiced defined the Vedic wisdom tradition in India.

The Vedic tradition did recognize that not all people are prepared enough to explore value education. So, they divided education in two tiers: higher education, *paravidya* in Sanskrit, education consisting of direct intuitive experience followed by conceptualization and embodiment that takes you beyond the limitations of the base level human condition; and lower education, *aparavidya* in Sanskrit, education that teaches you practical things for worldly survival and treats the values as information—only as rote rules and rituals to follow. In this way, you are allowed to maintain ignorance more or less and the level you live is influenced much more by the base-level human condition than the rote values and rituals.

In this way, higher education in the Indian tradition was really for people who wanted to satisfy higher needs—explore the creative arts, explore how to be ethical and teach people the rules for being ethical, how to be fair to others and bring justice to the world, how to heal themselves and others, how to explore and entertain as well as educate people via poetry and music. There were even people of higher education who wanted to explore truth including the truth about us, Who am I? There was even higher education that teaches you how to progressively reach higher and higher states of consciousness with increasing wholeness and happiness—*ananda* in Sanskrit.

Wisdom traditions similar in spirit to the original version of India albeit not so elaborate were discovered and developed in other places as well, In China, in Greece, in the Middle East.

One shortcoming of the higher/lower division of education was the denigration of the world. Because the best talents of the day naturally were attracted more to the higher education, the exploration of Consciousness and the archetypes got much more attention that the exploration of the material environment. In time, there was a tendency to regard the exploration of the material world as the pursuit of illusory trivia, *tuchhchho,* in Sanskrit. The other contributing factor to this attitude was the unavailability of the technology needed to explore the mysteries of the material world. That which we cannot explore, we denigrate.

Nevertheless, it is this kind of higher education that has given us what we call civilization. Obviously, it had transformative power over people and society that enabled parts of humanity to overcome the limits of the based-level condition.

This is the key. Transformation. Transformed people do not look down upon people who are not transformed because everyone has the potentiality. These people's time has not come yet (they need more reincarnation). In this way, wisdom tradition did not create any higher-lower education division.

But invariably, like the Indus valley civilization, every subsequent civilization in India and other parts of the world has the same history: ascent and descent. How does the descent happen?

How Religions became Elitist

Generally speaking, human history shows that all wisdom traditions eventually degenerate into religion; the original idealism is practiced more and more within a set of dogmas. Ordinary people were no longer free for creative exploration of the archetypes.

In India, higher education was reserved for people on a hereditary basis giving the caste system—brahmins and non-brahmins.

Thus, the religions compromised higher education, especially its transformative aspects, first, with various dogmatic misinterpretations of the ideas and practices, and second, the use of heredity to decide who gets higher education. In retrospect, we know now, that genes have not much to do with talent; talent is reincarnational. The old traditions assumed that people tend to take rebirth in the same families. While this is true for un-transformed people, the data shows that the more people transform, the more they become adventurous, and stray outside, first of their family, then of their community, finally, even of their country to take rebirth.

Furthermore, meditative exploration of the archetypal values in search of Oneness was difficult, the process was not completely known. So, the consensus grew that maybe only a few people can do it because they are so designated by Oneness, like appointing a son as your heir. Call Oneness as God and call these people as sons of God or God's avatar or messenger.

Of course, each religion would have only one or few such "sons of God," people who provide the inspiration behind that religion and the profound changes that become necessary.

The biggest dogma was infallibility of the scriptures that the sons of God or avatars developed and approved. You cannot challenge the infallibility of the Gospel truth and stay within the religion.

The archetypal values, under the religious dogma of God and son of God, became more like doctrines to practice and rituals to engage in, not ideas to explore and discover their truth for yourself, and then practice. In other words, religions taught *apara vidya* with dogmas to create even more ignorance.

These limitations allowed an elite group to maintain power by manipulating the rest. These limitations also produced less and less success in the embodiment of the values. Pretention and hypocrisy became common. Gradually, further corruption entered due to the unaddressed limitations of the base-level human condition, no doubt.

Elitism in Science

In the sixteenth century, the spirit of free exploration of wisdom was rekindled in the form of modern science with the avowed purpose of directly discovering the Truth about reality, not following scriptures blindly. The strategy was simple, and the technology was ready. Discover the truth as ideas, build theories, but then verify the theories with actual experiments.

We could not neither do experiment with Consciousness centuries ago nor did we have quantum theory to help theory-building about consciousness; but we could do both with inanimate matter! Science has been highly successful in deciphering the truth about inanimate matter and its movement with its two-prong strategy; but the success stalled when it came to explaining the human values and the nature of life and Consciousness.

The first hint of corruption erupted in the late nineteen hundreds. The great Darwin wrote his monumental book *The origin of species* in 1857. The philosopher Herbert Spencer coined the phrase survival of the fittest to explain Darwin's choice of naming the process of natural selection that settles which hereditary mutation will keep and which won't as the environment changed to which the species had to adapt. When genes were discovered and a few other things were clarified that had to be unified, materialist biologists did a trick that is still playing on us in a major way. They identified survival as a cause (some living molecules have survival instinct, an unverified assumption to this day), not a purpose.

Behold! As a material cause, survival has to be a material property. Obviously, ordinary molecules do not make any attempts to survive. So, the biologists made the assertion that the complex macromolecules of life—DNA, RNA, the proteins—they strive to survive. They also predicted that these molecules will be produced in the laboratory to prove the point of their causal origin.

But you know what? After decades of research, none of these macromolecules of life have been produced in the lab from scratch; their production depends on human researchers cleverly using enzymes (proteins) and/or some seed RNA.

Survival is not a cause, it is a purpose, a low ego-level purpose to be differentiated from high level purpose that religions call divine purpose.

Beginning with the nineteen fifties and sixties, the corruption hit science again. Power-play entered and dogma replaced the search for Truth. Why not declare that which we cannot presently understand—life, Consciousness, values—are epiphenomena of matter as well; the exact nature of the mechanism behind the epiphenomena will be discovered in some future—promissory materialism. As the psychologist Abraham Maslow said, if you have only a hammer in your hand, it is too tempting to see the world as nails.

Civilization was going downhill due to the religious dogmas for a long time; for a while, modern science brought back the spirit of creativity and discovery of Truth. The laws of science are based on the idea of absolute Truth—the archetype; they are not relative laws we create to dictate the ways of running a civilized society. Under materialist dogma, truth became relative, and scientific laws, science itself lost credibility.

Science with dogma has begun the decline of civilization once again all over the world. Science's dogma discredits religion as humbug, spiritual experiences notwithstanding. In this way, science not only lost credibility with people of spirituality/religion but became religion's enemy as it was centuries ago. The revenge of religion is to discredit science. Science started misinformation (matter is everything; spirituality and values do not exist, what are these doctrines but misinformation?); followers of religion spread misinformation about science even more effectively.

If you see all this, if you want to do something about it, there is good news for you in what this book brings you—quantum higher education.

Quantum Physics, Consciousness, and Higher Education

Quantum physics is the physics of possibilities for Consciousness to choose from. Consciousness, once more, is recognized as the ground of being and not only physical/material objects are acknowledged as quantum possibilities of Consciousness but also nonphysical/nonmaterial objects. Consciousness chooses from all these possibilities to create the manifest world of experience. There is no manifest world outside of the experiences of living and sentient beings.

What is Consciousness? Three characteristics define it:

1. It is an unconscious existence: the ground of being and its physical and nonphysical possibilities. With its causal power of choice.

2. When manifest, Consciousness becomes a subject-object awareness, a subject looking at objects.

3. During the course of manifest existence, Consciousness acquires ignorance (necessary to produce a substantial amount of forgetfulness of its true nature) and becomes constricted. This constricted condition is our familiar ego or me-centeredness. With education, with the explora-

tion and embodiment of the archetypes, we can acquire expanded states of consciousness (and remember!) that is experienced as happiness.

Let's summarize the most important message of quantum physics and the quantum science of Consciousness to higher education:

1. *Emphasis on Consciousness.* The world of creative manifestation consists of purposive movements of nonlocal Consciousness revealed moment to moment in the present centered creative experiences of a sentient being. There are also conditioned manifestations driven by ego's purpose. These two drives have to be balanced. The first one is called holotropy; it takes us toward wholeness. The second is called hylotropy; this one takes us to more and more separateness. The psychologist Stan Grof has enunciated these drives in this appropriate way.

2. *Emphasis on choice and free will.* It is very important to recognize that consciousness is primarily needed to choose among quantum possibilities so that the possibility wave can collapse and manifest the world. Even in the ego, we maintain some freedom of choice: first, from among a spectrum of conditioned alternatives; second, the choice to say no to conditioning altogether to opt for creative freedom.

In the early days of consciousness research, some researchers—physicists all—attempted to theorize that consciousness is the unified field behind all material forces, so squeamish were they of the idea that consciousness uses choice, not a force, for making changes. A Psychologist, David Hawking, however, had no problem seeing this which he elucidated in a beautiful book called *Power vs. Force.*

3. *Emphasis on purpose and values.* The purpose of the movement of Consciousness is to satisfy first the survival needs and then higher needs defined by the archetypes: Abundance, Power, Beauty, Love, Goodness, Truth, Justice, Wholeness, and all that. Both needs are important.

Human development from our prehistorical beginnings has been a movement toward the exploration of higher needs creating civilizations. However, whenever the exploration of higher needs became lopsided ignoring the survival needs, civilizations declined.

Human societies today are dangerously moving toward the emphasis of survival needs ignoring higher needs creating chaos. In this emphasis, higher education has degenerated into job training. We desperately need to reorient higher education, restore the pursuit of higher needs, and ensure the continuation of higher purpose of human development.

While higher education engages in educating people so that they embody the archetypes and act as producers in new business enterprises of subtle products (of meaning and value), lower education will engage in creating a new consumer society of people who will be initiated into the exploration of higher needs via consumption.

Are we ready for this? Don't doubt it. It is not a coincidence that robots are taking over all routine jobs that today's people of lower education engage in. What will these people do except to participate in the subtle economy as both producers and consumers?

4. *Emphasis on nonphysical software.* There is no need for epiphenomenalism, emergence of life and meaning from the movement of matter. We have developed computers now. We know computers give us hardware, but we have to supply them mind-created software to use them for

our purpose. So, realize this: The human being consists of both material hardware and nonmaterial vital and mental software. More on this later.

Hardware science ends up with deterministic laws for bulk matter; they are objective and largely independent of our worldview. It is not so for our software which has both conditioned and creative aspects. It is the association with quantum software and its blueprints that makes the hardware quantum occasionally and allows Consciousness access for choice and collapse of its possibilities into actuality, as needed.

Higher education must include not only the physical and mechanical side of the human being (hard sciences—physics and chemistry, and technology including biotech) but also the nonphysical and creative side of the human (soft sciences—the consciousness side of biology, health sciences, psychology and social sciences, economics, and business).

5. *Attitudinal change.* Balancing the drives of holotropy and hylotropy implies that there needs to be an attitudinal change from exclusively lower (as now) or exclusively higher needs (as in the spiritual/religious eras) to a balance of lower and higher needs. This also implies a balance of the tendency to remain in conditioning and the tendency for creativity.

To reflect this attitudinal change in higher education, our educational pursuits must undergo radical change:

i. Health science must restrain its current preoccupation with disease and cure and morph into a science of health and wellbeing, disease prevention, and healing all in the pursuit of wholeness. And wholeness here must include the healing of our experiences of not only sensing (physical body) but also feeling (vital body), thinking (mental body) and intuiting (archetypal also called supramental body). Wholeness at each level of experience must also achieve a balance of creativity and conditioning—spirit and the ego.

ii. Likewise, psychology and psychiatry must give up the preoccupation with mental disease and pleasure and its abuses and morph into a science of happiness. Because the journey to increasing levels of happiness involves dealing with shadows at each level, psychotherapists with knowledge of both mental disorder as well as mental order would be better guides of human search of happiness.

iii. Economics and business administration must give up their preoccupation with material wealth and morph into a science of prosperity in the pursuit of the archetype of abundance along with goodness.

iv. In a similar vein, politicians must be taught to pursue the archetype of power in conjunction with the archetype of goodness so that they can use their personal power to empower the people that elect them, into office.

v. Law education must be supplemented by creative exploration of the archetype of Justice on the part of law practitioners and judges. This will enable a much-needed revision of the criminal justice system operating now which is grossly unfair for the lower echelon of the society. This will restore respect for law once again.

vi. Scientists must go back to the spirit of truth-seeking science and explore the archetype of truth in their trade.

vii. Religious and spiritual teachers must explore and embody the archetype of goodness. This way goodness and ethical dealing becomes a categorical imperative (a language used by the philosopher Immanuel Kant) and the teachers can do no wrong, they can walk their talk.

viii. Educationists must explore the archetype of wholeness. This is a long affair, and embodiment will be gradual. Quantum educationists will have to have completed at least the embodiment of the archetype of abundance, goodness, and truth.

A feeling of abundance is necessary because teaching cannot be directly connected to a profit motif and therefore, teacher's pay would always be relatively low. Moral education is important from the get-go; so, teachers have to be able to walk their talk about ethics. And the exploration of the archetype of truth is essential to have access to transcendent truth that transcends the duality of truth and lie.

The pursuit of wholeness involves the archetype of power as well. The healers and educationists will need to learn how to use the personal power to empower their clients.

All this involves what mythology calls hero's journey (see later). In the rest of the book, we will further elaborate on the basic premises of hero's journey as higher education—quantum style.

One more thing. When we are in our ego, the ego reigns supreme. Choice, purpose, need, all is governed by the ego (consciousness goes along with it). However, the ego can always say no to conditioning. In this way, quantum education crucially depends on inspiration; the ego has to be inspired to say no to conditioning and be open to higher purpose and higher needs.

The Challenges of Lower Education and the Lower/Higher Divide of Today: Understanding the Science of Child Development

The challenge of lower education has always been this: the understanding of child development; and we never had this understanding in full until quantum science came along. In spiritual societies of the old, they understood the important role of the quantum self, meaning and purpose but tended to undermine ego development; the brain was pretty much a black box then. Neuroscience has made good progress on gathering empirical data on the brain, but because of the materialist prejudice of the researchers, developmental psychology is biased toward making it all a matter of ego development—only rational ego at that. Leaving out the role of intuition, creativity, meaning and archetypes on one hand and that of feelings and emotions on the other hand has had disastrous consequence on children and teen education; among other things this has given us the lower educated—higher educated divide.

When we develop a quantum theory of child development, we find that healthy adult personalities should fall into nine types. These personality types called enneagrams were first discovered perhaps empirically in wisdom traditions. This typology clearly demonstrates that development strongly depends on how children are allowed to process feelings and emotions on one hand, and the intuitions and the spiritual on the other hand.

The enneagram is divided in three personality groups each containing three types of personality. These groups are aptly named Body centered, Heart centered, and Head centered. The reason for the labelling is self-explanatory. Both the body-centered group and the Heart-centered group focus more on feelings in the body for their internal processing rather the rational mind. In this way, the current emphasis of education on rational mind alone does a gross disservice for these people, many of whom are women. Some women compromise, give up feminine values, and opt for men's choice—rational mind—for internal processing. This shortchanges the original goal of the feminist movement to bring feminine values—love and related emotions—into our social institutions. This will not stand.

Body centered people—men and women—prefer street smart practical but value-based thinking rather than the ivory-tower often detached-from-reality rational thinking of intellectuals.

Quantum education brings feminine values as well as archetypal values in education and sets education in the right gear.

CHAPTER 3

Bad News and Good News on the Education Front

To summarize the discussion once again: Starting in the later part of the twentieth century education changed into information processing and job training. Why? Because of a power struggle between people of science that want materialism and people of religion that want old tradition of feudalism to continue, eventually leading to the worldview polarization that has divided politics and culture across the world ever since.

In the struggle for power, science has antithetically morphed from a search for Truth into a science with the dogma of scientific materialism—an artifice to make everything-is-matter philosophy appear scientific. Materialism—all is matter—is an old philosophy. The science establishment now claims that science has given scientific validity to this philosophy, because this is the way the world is—all *is* matter.

Yes, this declaration—everything is matter—a straightjacket for science to wear, has made many prejudicial ideas of religion look ridiculous and has certainly helped loosen the stranglehold of those ideas on societies. Ideas like God as a super-duper king of kings sitting on a throne in outer space, and you-go-to-heaven if you are good and hell if you do evil.

Agreed, some of the ideas that religions have propagated over millennia are too simplistic. A glaring example is the idea of hell of eternal fire and brimstone where bad people go after death as their punishment. They are dead, they have no physical body to suffer from physical fire and brimstone!

The idea of hell is good riddance, no doubt. But to ideate that human beings are machines with no need of ethics is as ridiculous as the idea of hell. It actually releases the agents of hell—the negative emotional brain circuits—in the human base-level condition. The idea creates hell on earth. Unleashed human negativity has created global climate change, ongoing war, readily available and indiscriminately used Internet pornography, unlimited greed leading to big business monopoly, rampant drug addiction. Are these things any worse than fire and brimstone?

Agreed some of this hell has always existed on our planet, Agreed that religions preach ethics, but the practitioners are hypocrites, they don't practice ethics. Is another form of hypocrisy the answer, passing dogma as truth?

Correcting one wrong by another wrong just misfires. There is no built-in punishment for being bad is correct, no doubt. But does that imply that there is no advantage of being good? But this is what humans-are-machines dogma is telling us.

Materialist science has undermined the whole question of ethics. Especially, what has hurt science itself is that undermining ethics and values also undermines the idea of absolute Truth. When truth becomes relative, first, you get Fox news and Donald Trump; but eventually fraud and misinformation in the practice of science itself.

Bottom line is this. Today, these materialist scientists complain how Trump and Fox News are creating chaos. But guess who started the chaos by undermining the value of truth? And guess who is already paying the price because there are scientists greedy enough to falsify data? These scientists are not aware that they are chopping off the very tree of truth-seeking science on which they sit?

Today in America, the liberal media blames all our problems on misinformation by those misguided people of the conservative opposition while continuing to ignore that they, too, are propagating misinformation by propagating materialism. Implicitly if not explicitly, by suppressing all the progress in post-materialist science for example.

How Materialist Higher Education Compromises the Education in What You are Most Interested in

What has hurt our culture the most is that although the ideas of science within materialism makes human beings into mechanical machines, half of the people in the USA and perhaps Europe and even the rest of the educated world has been manipulated into believing materialist science and implicitly accepting that they are machines. It would be easy to say that this happened only through sophistry and through the help from the liberal media and politicians, and through information technology, but that would be wrong. Materialist science's biggest allure is that its message is a permissive society; it gives people permission to cater to their tendencies of base-level conditioning. Moreover, it delivers technology to help people express these base-level tendencies.

In the seventies, a group of Japanese tourists came to America in search of the permissive society; they thought that there must be an organization explaining how it works. They were so curious, they wanted to know more so that they could import the idea to Japan. This is one of the way, materialism sold itself all over the world.

However, the archetypes may appear superfluous in view of the banishment of God, heaven, and hell, a substantial number of people even today discover real value in exploring and embodying them—albeit only a little. Furthermore, there are certain positive stuff like altruism, maternal love, and romance, that are almost instinctual and universal in people's lives. Additionally, there are the talented and gifted who are naturally drawn to creativity; even materialist science needs their help. All this breeds confusion even among the practitioners of scientific materialism about its validity.

Philosophy came to the rescue in the form of existentialism—existence precedes essence or values. In other words, human being first; values are human created. Since they are human created, they are not binding, like human created laws. Violating the human laws and being caught will get people in trouble, but they can get around the laws and never get caught for it. They still need to pretend however and pose as law-abiding citizens.

Thus the idea of political correctness: values have no scientific basis but we must pretend as if they are not only in words but also in superficial public behavior. The implicit understanding is that you don't have to go by the values in private dealings; in privacy you have permission to let your negative emotions hang out. And then you protect privacy as your fundamental right. Talk about having your cake and eating it too.

But of course, pretended good behavior does not enable people to curb their negative emotions; hence "greed is good" or "power-at-all-cost" mindset dominate society.

Since they created all this wonderful cover for the rest of academia, the architects of materialist science dominate all education especially higher education. There is a clear hierarchy in higher education institutions. Hard sciences dominate; they are the legal authority of what is valid and what is not. Hard sciences then dictate how the soft and social sciences should be, and what they should not be. The liberal arts, what was the central theme of "higher" education at a previous time, is the lowest in the totem pole now.

In the previous era of modernism, a liberal arts graduate could enter any profession (except hard science and technology) because her degree guaranteed the ability of meaning processing—mental intelligence in any area she would choose to explore. Now, there is no high paying job prospect for the liberal arts student because he has been trained only for a job in fine arts, or literature, or music, or history, depending on his specialization.

The infrastructure of a materialist society runs on industry and high tech. The education in the hard sciences remain useful and pays off too if you can find a job. The vast underbelly of industry and high tech consists of unskilled labor who do not require higher education. Due to automation, the scope of job-oriented higher education in these areas is shrinking rapidly.

The vast demand of "higher education" by whatever definition is in the soft human sciences. Among the human sciences that are shortchanged the most under materialism are also soft sciences: the health sciences, psychology, economics, and social sciences including politics. Think about this. Under scientific materialism, healing is replaced by curing the physical symptoms of disease; psychotherapy becomes counselling about how to cope with mental disorder in the short term, economics becomes the exploration of how to grow material wealth for a person or a corporation, not abundance and well-being in society; politics becomes the art of accumulating power for oneself. You never get a glimpse of the transcendent wholeness beyond health and disease, mental order and disorder or happiness and suffering, prosperity and poverty, and democracy and autocracy.

What is taught in the soft sciences under the materialist dogma is not entirely useless if you believe the materialists' claim—people are what they are, they cannot change; human beings do have a mechanical side to them. But that is not what defines health or prosperity or happiness. So, materialists equate health with absence of disease; and what is taught as health science is disease management science which concentrates on drugs and surgical technology with disastrous consequence to health care cost. Similarly, science of prosperity becomes the science of absence of poverty, and the poverty-avoiding mindset unleashes unruly greed that destroys society. Finally, science of happiness degenerates into science of curing mental disorder.

According to materialist science, the only way the positive can come to us is via mechanical molecules of pleasure. Logic then says why not enhance pleasure through other external mechanical means, why be limited by biology? If computers can enhance our mind, why not let drugs enhance our body's performance? This leads to drug addiction and abuse again with disastrous consequences to society.

Materialists argue, making human beings more efficient consuming machines has been good for creating unprecedented amounts of technological products and this has created much material wealth as well. Never mind the loss of freedom of people to choose. Never mind that some of these products are unhealthy. Never mind that the consumer economy is majorly responsible for global climate change. Never mind that most scientific materialist research today goes to making weapons and that leads to war.

We have paid a very heavy price for all this, and it is not just carbon emission in the atmosphere and global climate change, or war and terrorism. Materialist science has made vast intelligent segments of the society—the artists, musicians, actors, sports people, and journalists into strugglers for survival; a few with name and fame are excepted. The social workers, the educationists, the political organizers who do not make it to the power elite, businesspeople who prefer to follow values instead of giving priority to amassing unnecessary wealth, and of course, the lower educated, also have become secondary citizens.

No doubt, all intelligent people are quite aware of the hypocrisy of religions. But to intelligent people, the hypocrisy of science within materialism should also be crystal clear: if there is no absolute truth, why should we trust science?

Yes, religion has lost much credibility, but a mechanical machine science applied to conscious and potentially creative human beings does not have much credibility either.

In circa 2020, Donald Trump held together a 95% of consensus among Republicans in the USA with his politics of lies with the lure of money and power; he did it with fear and the charisma of money and power. The materialist science establishment is holding together a much bigger consensus of scientists all over the world by a science based on a dogma, everything is matter, everything is mechanical, a lie with the lure of a permissive society and pleasure-enhancing technology defying the value-constraints of spiritual traditions. This consensus is also a consensus only among materialist scientists while they are on the job; it too, is a consensus of fear and the charisma created by power and money.

Know this. Just as today in USA we are seeing many Republicans retired from positions of power quickly find their voice against Trumpism back, retired scientists quickly discover spirituality, the metaphysical foundation of religion.

In this environment of relative truth and fear, we cannot educate any more in the traditional transformational way because people do not know any more which knowledge, whose truth is the light that transforms ignorance. In this way, education has become transactional, mere processing of information (without value judgment, without ascribing meaning) and of course job training.

The Good News: The Truth-seeking Spirit of Science is Alive and Well

To the intelligent, conscientious explorers of life, all the above is very bad news.

Is there any good news? This question always reminds me of a story. A man develops a gangrene in his right leg so serious that it has to be amputated. The operation is performed. When the patient regains consciousness, the surgeon appears and says, "I have some bad news and some good news. The patient waits in anticipation, what can be bad about such a straightforward operation? That's what they told him before the operation, the operation is routine.

The surgeon continues, "I may as well tell you the bad news first. We chopped off the wrong leg."

Naturally, the patient is devastated. Seeing his face in the throw of despair, the surgeon now assures him, "Don't be upset. I have good news too. The gangrene in your surviving leg is not as bad as we originally thought." The story is funny because the "good" news is really not so great!

The people who are looking for some solutions, the good news that is not so greatis this. The scientific materialists notwithstanding, the dogma-free spirit of science is very much alive in many active scientists and thanks to them a series of new scientific developments have emerged. The new developments expose the weaknesses of scientific materialism, and these scientists search for alternative post-materialist paradigms. There are new paradigms based on the philosophy of holism and systems theory that venture outside verifiable science or at best be considered borderline promissory science. There are also paradigms that declare primacy of Consciousness but then succumb to dualism of subjective and objective science. Dualism is not a viable alternative to scientific materialism.

You can think of all these attempts as attempts to fix the gangrene of the patient in our story above. These attempts are demonstratively inconsistent and ad hoc. A full discussion is beyond the scope of this book.

Quantum science changes the metaphysical foundation of science. Instead of doing science with the primary-of-matter ontology, quantum physics opens the door for science within the primacy of consciousness. The gangrene of scientific materialism must go; this is what quantum physics and experimental data are saying to us. There is no way around it unless you play the game of denial as the materialists are doing.

The Scope of Quantum Physics

The real good news is this. Newtonian physics has now been replaced by a more inclusive view—quantum physics—that holds for both submicroscopic and macroscopic realms of physics. Quantum physics explains all of physics and chemistry. When quantum physics is seriously applied to the movement of single objects it unambiguously morphs into a new paradigm of science called quantum science—science within the primacy of consciousness—that expands the power of quantum physics to explain all the previously unexplained phenomena of biology, psychology, and all other human sciences. Quantum science adds to mechanistic science all the new ideas needed to treat the human being beyond its conditioned ego homeostasis burdened by the base-level human condition—Consciousness, nonphysical energies of life, mental meaning, and purposive archetypes including ethics and moral values—to adequately deal with the nonmechanical and creative aspects of the human being.

It should not be surprising that quantum physics and quantum science are a science of Consciousness because of course, it is Consciousness that is an everyday reminder to every intelligent person that mechanistic materialist science is only half of the story and may not even be the important half any more for investigation and exploration because that job is already mostly done. Yes, we know our mechanical side pretty well.

From Quantum Mechanics to Quantum Physics, to Quantum Science

Quantum mechanics consists of completely mechanistic equations of movement (the Schrödinger equation) that enables us to calculate mathematically and deterministically, the possible motions of submicroscopic objects—elementary particles of matter and energy. The elementary particle of energy is called a quantum, hence the name quantum mechanics.

However, the catch is that what quantum mechanics calculates are waves of possibility. You can calculate the probabilities associated with each possibility. That's good enough when you have the movement of many objects to consider. But it leaves open the question: if the world consists of possibility, how can we have manifest experiences?

So, we need to generalize quantum *mechanics* to quantum *physics*: quantum mechanics plus quantum measurement theory. Empirically, measurement, our observation, converts the waves of possibility into particles of actuality. The theory of quantum measurement is necessary to make sense of quantum mechanics, to apply quantum mechanics to explaining experimental data.

Note however: quantum physics becomes deterministic once again if we adopt the probabilistic interpretation: probabilities of events can be calculated from quantum mechanics alone. Therefore, for large number of objects or systems of objects, quantum physics can be used in a mechanistic way. In this way, traditional physics, chemistry, and hard technological applications of quantum physics is basically quantum mechanics. This is indeed what is taught in our university and is completely kosher.

For a single object though we must acknowledge that the object is bundle of possibilities for Consciousness to choose from. Behold! Consciousness is a being with causality: it is the causal agent of change from possibility to actuality. In this way, it is the creator of the manifest world. Consciousness chooses out of the (coherent) super-position of many possibilities offered by the object a unique actuality.

Example: for an electron, quantum mechanics calculates a (coherent) superposition of possibilities of being at many positions of space at once (like a wave). Conscious choice collapses the wave (many positions at once) into a particle (one unique position at a given time).

Quantum physics, when applied to the movement of single objects and/or events, leads us to a science of nonmaterial Consciousness—a unique being of potential Oneness, a being of possibility that becomes both manifest subject and object of an experience upon measurement, a being of both material and nonmaterial possibilities. In the movements of our lives, we are primarily interested in our individual movements. In general, individual movements are important to consider in our science of biology, psychology, and all social sciences.

The extension of quantum physics of the material to both material and nonmaterial possibilities of Consciousness we call quantum science. This is what we need additionally for building the quantum science of biology, physiology and health, psychology, and all social affairs.

Implications for Quantum Education

Before scientific materialism came about, it is the mechanical side of the human being that intelligent people recognized as ignorance and education was to enable the human being to acquire the knowledge that would free him/her from shackles of machine-being (animal being too) and explore the rest of his or her being lying in potentiality and embody the potentiality into actuality.

Educational research was the search for that knowledge knowing which you can find answers to all your problems of living. That knowledge is now revealed in the form of a science of Consciousness. So, higher education can return to its proper role. And lower education as well.

There is another piece of good news, too. Polarization has not been good for our societies and culture; we are on the verge of a breakdown of civilization. The new quantum science of Consciousness, by establishing Consciousness and values as scientific, integrates the spiritual/religious essence of reality with its material essence, and in this way, spirituality and science.

This integration of science with the wisdom traditions should restore the credibility of science as well. The new science, being a science of Consciousness, expands the two prongs—theory and experiment—of traditional science into three prongs—theory, experiment, and experience. Likewise, on the application side, besides material technology, we can look forward to spiritual technology that invests human capital to make progress.

In practical terms, materialist science remains intact under the new science in the fields of the hard sciences dealing with the nonliving: physics, chemistry, engineering, etc. Materialists have nothing to fear. It is the science of the domain of the living that gets the re-visioning.

Hierarchy of Needs

An important point to note is this: it is the human sciences dealing with health, psychology, economics, etc. that requires a contextual and attitudinal change. So long we stay within the boundaries of the base-level human condition, materialist science is right: we are dominated by survival needs. However, you should note that even survival is not really a material cause, it is a conscious purpose. When in the survival mode, we explore archetypes—abundance, power, beauty, and wholeness—all dedicated to the survival of the material body. What's the difference in this change in attitude? Even the lower need archetypes of survival become transpersonal devoted to higher needs: we seek wealth to explore and find abundance that include others and satisfies; we seek power to prove our worth to others while empowering them; we seek beauty to find happiness beyond bodily pleasure; we seek wholeness in our inner experience as well.

The idea of "higher" education is not to enable people to get higher economic status in the society but to enable people how to satisfy their higher needs beyond mere survival, the need for exploring meaning and purposeful values. It is these higher needs that is the contextual change that quantum transformational education addresses: it not only educates you for better performance in your profession but also teaches how-to live in synchrony with what you learn to think.

In the new approach the science of medicine becomes the science of health once again, not of disease and curing disease. The science of economics becomes the true science of prosperity where the goal is the mind set of abundance transcending the mindset of poverty. And the science of psychology becomes the authentic science of happiness expanding beyond its traditional preoccupation with psychopathology.

Well, ok, you say; it sounds like, this education will teach me a lot of new intellectual albeit scientific concepts to get a new perspective on fields of human profession that have become transactional. But how does that help us to actually manifest health, prosperity and happiness in our lives and help others to do the same?

Good question. Quantum science also gives us a science of manifestation. It does not work for manifesting pleasure toys if that's what you are interested in. But the science works wonders with manifesting health, prosperity, and happiness once you get its new archetypal perspective. And yes, this is part and parcel of quantum education: how to live your quantum way of thinking, how to manifest meaning and values in your life including health, prosperity, and happiness. Since you will be taught how to walk your talk, the quality of your service to your clients in those professions will also show a dramatic increase.

Quantum science is the future for assessing, exploring, and embodying the potentialities of the human being, of what we can be, what is higher education can transform us into. The wisdom traditions were an early glimpse of the scope of the future of humanity. They laid out how they saw as the ideal human; their philosophy is sometimes called idealism. The ideal human explores and embodies the ideals—the archetypes.

You have never heard of idealism or archetypes before reading this book, you say. Well, Consciousness and its exalted qualifications such as meaning and archetypes were discovered by ancient people starting with the Indians; it was independently discovered in China, Greece, and the middle East. Most notable among these discoverers are Krishna, Buddha, Lao Tzu, Socrates, Plato, the Kabbalists in Israel, Jesus, and Mohammad. World's civilizations grew around the teachings of these people. Where did these teachings go? They still live in esoteric wisdom traditions. But most people today do not know that; instead, they think these people created those dogma-infested systems called religions.

Materialists sell the belief that what we can sense is what is real, a belief system called realism. They decry idealism and ideals as unrealistic pursuits for human beings to waste their time. Get real and enjoy the condition you have, eat, drink, earn a living to enjoy more and more objects of merriment.

But there is nothing idealistic about quantum science's re-visioning of the ideals. *It comes with the science of how to explore and manifest the ideals in our manifest being.* When we explore and embody the ideals, that is, the archetypal values, the ideals become real. The realism-idealism dichotomy is a false dichotomy.

CHAPTER 4

Quantum Educationist: It Is Important for You to Understand the Debate Points in the Ongoing Battle of Worldviews

At the risk of repeating, in this chapter we further elaborate the worldview debate and how it is affecting education. We will begin with spiritual value-education that quantum physics is elaborating and proposing to restore. We will discuss why ordinary people get confused and how to prevent confusion with today's quantum insights. We will then discuss how religions distort and compromise spiritual education. Finally, we will discuss how materialists managed to deny value education completely and the quantum way out.

The Vision of the Wisdom traditions that Quantum Science is Restoring and why People Misunderstand

It behooves us to appreciate how much of the quantum ideas discovered today the early explorers of consciousness were able to envision as they laid out their model of higher education.

The basic premise of spiritual wisdom traditions is this: Higher education has to bring the light of knowledge that removes the darkness of ignorance of the base level human condition. In the olden days, ignorance meant the nature of the self; today, in quantum science ignorance means ignorance of human potentialities in general. If this latter interpretation resonates with you, you will ask, What other way is there to think of education? Shouldn't everyone think this way about education?

No, everyone does not think that way. This way of thinking about education presumes some features of us that are very much out of synch with ordinary human ego stuck in the base-level condition. This is what religionists and materialists exploit.

- *Consciousness.* People are conscious; they can distinguish themselves from the environment as having a self, separate from the objects of the environment in their experience.

Yes, all humans including common people do that, but they don't necessarily see it that way. They take it for granted. This is where the me-centeredness is such as a blinder. When you see yourself as me, an object, it is the same as other people see you, as another me. But why is your me-ness so special to you that you think everything is about you?

The other end of the confusion is revealed by the often-asked question, this one from religious minded people, Is a rock conscious? Isn't God everywhere and in everything? If Consciousness is the scientific name for God, shouldn't a rock be conscious? These people cannot distinguish between unconscious and conscious, Consciousness and manifest awareness. They cannot understand the distinction of the subject-experiencer 'I' and the object 'me.'

The educationist has to accept that although people are conscious, they are confused about it. Now that we have a science of Consciousness, a priority of education—lower and higher—is to clarify the confusion. The world of manifestation consists of purposive movements of Consciousness revealed moment to moment in the experiences of sentient beings. The purpose is to satisfy first the survival needs and then higher needs defined by the archetypes: Truth, Love, Justice, Wholeness, and all that.

Human development from our prehistorical beginnings has been a movement toward the exploration of higher needs. Human societies today are dangerously moving toward the emphasis of only survival needs creating chaos. It is the job of higher education to restore and ensure the continuation of the pursuit of higher purpose of human development.

- *Meaning.* The self, aware of itself, can process meaning, can discern darkness and light, ignorance and wisdom, can discern ambiguity of meaning, can distinguish between real meaning and organized meaning or information.

Human beings lose this power of distinction between meaning and information because of authorities in our growing up period. Our parents and our schoolteachers have such aura of authority, and they are so eager to tell their protege the meaning of everything, we pick up the belief early on that meaning is identical as programed meaning—information, doesn't everyone give the same meaning to everything? Cultural anthropology has been helpful in exposing this ignorance of the base level human condition.

A corollary of the same ignorance prompted a Nobel laureate neuroscientist to seriously propose that there is a one-to-one correspondence between objects of the world and the meaning we give it. You see, then meaning becomes objective; then it is a plausible ability of the brain. This scientist must have never encountered a metaphor!

- *Feeling.* Because of the base-level human condition and the current materialist worldview emphasis on material sensing and mental information, people are confused about pure feelings that do arise in conjunction of body organs other than the brain cortex. Like the character Mr. Duffy created by novelist James Joyce, most people live today "at a little distance from the body."

Confusion is also created because we most often experience emotions—feelings mixed up with thoughts. Materialists only talk about emotions, a clever strategy. Educators must be aware that quantum science gives us a theory of feeling that agrees with everybody's experience—the chakras (fig. 3).

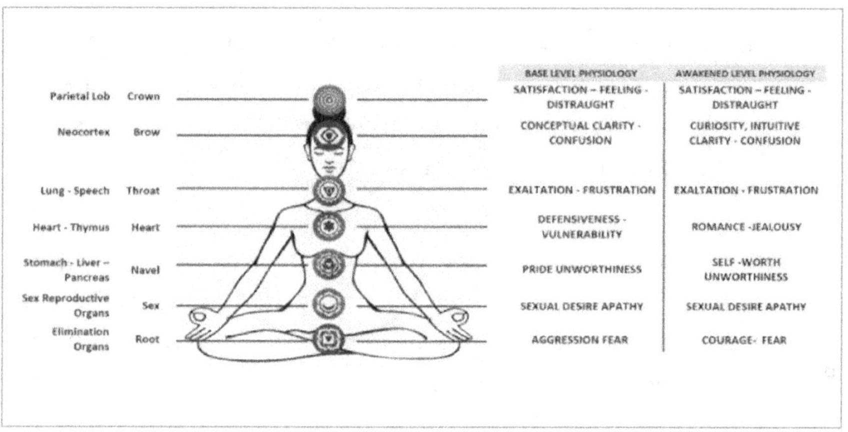

Figure 3. The Chakras are depicted with their associated organs shown on the extreme left; on the right we display the feelings at each of the chakras both for ordinary egos and for awakened selves. The top feeling at each chakra signifies the feeling when the organs are functioning properly, and the bottom signifies the feeling when the organ function is blocked.

- *Intuitions.* Are there other possibilities of Consciousness that we experience? We discover scientific laws as truth that governs the universe somehow. This is an intuitive thought—intuition and thought together, intuition given meaning in the form of thought. Or intuitions cognized as intuitive thought. Where do intuitions come from? They are quantum messages from Consciousness about its purposive archetypal values. Indeed, we recognize our intuitions as the source of what we recognize as human values. These objects of intuition are the archetypes.

We experience intuitions in another way. Mothers among us have a special experience with their babies, an intuitive feeling of oneness and expansion that comes with intense caring for the other; they call these feelings love. Men too experience such feelings episodically when they are "in love," these episodes are called romance. In this way, we see that these intuitions can be represented or cognized both as thoughts and as feelings and of course simultaneously as emotions.

Higher education must include not only the physical and mechanical side of the human being (hard sciences—physics and chemistry, technology including biotech) but also the nonphysical and creative side of the human (soft sciences—the conscious side of biology, health sciences, psychology, economics, and business).

- *Purpose.* Meaning processing is not only a causal response but also a purposive response.

This may be a cognitive difficulty to accept only for the materialist scientist. After four centuries of living with David Hume's ghost—causality—they really think that all-purpose are appearances of purpose, not real. Indeed, biologists *en masse* label the philosophy of purpose—teleology—as teleonomy—appearance of purpose. A physicist had to point out to them in an article in *Scientific American* in 1963 that the fossil data has a one-way-ness from simple to complex giving us the biological arrow of time—the distinction of past from the future which is a definitive proof that evolution has purpose. Physical cause conserves the two-way-ness of time. This may not be obvious; but it is a fact that both Newton's equation and quantum equation for the movement of objects does not distinguish between time past and time future. The one-way-ness exhibited by the fossil data can only be produced by purposiveness of evolution—evolution proceeds with the purpose of more complexity so as to enable the processing of higher and higher needs.

- *Free will.* The self can choose to respond to the light of knowledge rather than stay in ignorance.

Authorities impose this ignorance on ordinary people by always telling them what do to. The denial of free will is where hypocrisy of the materialist scientist shows up the most. Quite a few scientists start as rebels against authority; how can they not know about free will at some level of Consciousness?

- *Creativity.* The self is creative. When called for and challenged by the experience of light it responds in a new way using creativity rather than stay in the known conditioned state of ignorance.

Creativity begins with the extrasensory perception of intuition. ESP, intuition, and creativity are some things materialists deny tooth and nail. Creativity theorists have found evidence of not only ESP but discontinuity in the creative process. This, too materialists deny and fight against tooth and nail.

- *Hierarchy of needs.* Given that when his or her base level need is fulfilled in his or her ignorant state, a human being can and do often opt for creative change implies that the human needs must extend beyond survival, that there is a whole hierarchy of needs that only progressive education can satisfy. Higher archetypal needs like love, truth, beauty, goodness, justice, and wholeness.

Impoverished people, most people of the olden days and a substantial majority even now, are too tied up with survival needs. But of course, it is one of the most amazing things about the base level human condition is this: even with affluence some people do not see beyond financial prosperity and power to dominate others.

Ideals like abundance and power that materialists do covet become transpersonal when explored with these higher needs in mind. Naturally materialists hold on to the belief that human beings have only survival needs like animals.

There needs to be an attitudinal change from lower needs to higher needs. The re-enchantment of twenty-first century people from "Newton's sleep," that has been threatening us from the seventeenth century and became the case with most people in the past decades, will need a major educational effort, a constant reminder and demonstration that consumption and production of objects of higher needs can be fun and eventually leads to stable and lasting health, prosperity, and happiness on the personal side and makes the society moral and just to boot. This can only be done by transformed people walking their talk.

To reflect this attitudinal change in higher education, i) health science must be taught as a science of health and wellbeing, disease prevention, and healing all in the pursuit of wholeness; ii) psychology and psychiatry must give up the preoccupation with mental disease and pleasure and its abuses and morph into a science of happiness; iii) economics must give up its preoccupation with material wealth and morph into a science of prosperity in the pursuit of the archetype of abundance.

- *Archetypes.* Where does the stimulus for the higher need come from? It comes from Consciousness in the form of stimuli called archetypes. Love, truth, etc. are these archetypes.

Archetypes, to this day, remain obscure to most people. If you consult Internet, you find ample signs of denial of the concept. Intuition is the experience through which consciousness sends us the archetypes. The evolutionary future of humanity demands that we make the shift from the current emphasis on rational mind to intuitive mind.

Because intuitions come to us via ESP, the materialist scientists fight against their existence tooth and nail. They try to sell the idea that what we call intuition is the result of having huge experience and memory of the move required to solve the problem without reasoning. This kind of "intuition may make a chess grandmaster, but it won't help you transform.

Education as removal of ignorance was motivated by an intuitive futuristic vision of the human being that is still unfolding. Misinformation on intuition is slowing down the unfolding.

- *Nonphysical software.* Except for a relatively small number of technologically oriented people, by and large, people deal with human software—lived memories of thinking and emotions, that's where it is at for most people. Yet, it is hard to comprehend the nonphysical for today's people after decades of living with materialist propaganda machine. Almost as hard as it was for people before Newton to think of objects in outer space in the same way as objects on earth. A major effort needs to be spent in emphasizing not only the nonphysical nature of human software and the physical nature of only the hardware but also the fact that both physical and nonphysical are potentialities of Consciousness to choose from.

Hardware science ends up with deterministic laws for bulk matter; they are objective and largely independent of our worldview. It is not so for our software which has both conditioned and creative aspects. let's elaborate on this further.

Revisit: Why is the Hardware Hard?

I hope you caught one message of whatever changes quantum physics is producing in our worldview. We are made of material hardware, bulk matter. The hardware follows the old deterministic laws of Newtonian vintage; it better be that way; we need a stable reference point for our body. Our hardware better be hard to change.

And yet, this can be disappointing and a little puzzling. After all, macro is made of micro in the material sector of reality, so if micro is quantum, shouldn't the macro be so too? A concept of waves called coherence helps you to understand the situation.

- *Coherence:* We have discussed coherence and decoherence before. Here is another way to introduce the subject. A possibility wave of an electron can be forced to become two identical waves of possibility of itself (as for example when passed through a double slitted screen); the two waves can interfere with each other. When collapsed on a photographic plate in bulk, we see the result of such "interference with itself"—an interference pattern of alternate bright (where the electrons fall) and dark (where no electron arrives) fringes. This abilities of being able to interfere with itself when split up is called coherence.

In this way, coherence of a bundle of waves of possibility is the bundle's ability of interfering with itself when split, demonstrating its wave nature. How big a bundle can do that? Recently, researchers have demonstrated that even large molecules containing 2000 atoms can split and interfere with itself. But don't forget that a kilogram of bulk matter contains 6.23 x 10 26 molecules. So, no one expects bulk matter to have quantum coherence for internal movements of its parts especially at room temperature. Although quantum movement persists for the external movement of the center of mass and the internal movement of individual parts.

Once again, Realize this: quantum mechanics predicts that for large masses, material objects become approximately Newtonian. Why? Two reasons: 1) the movement becomes deterministic and objective; the movement of the center of mass is minuscule, us subjects cannot see it with naked eyes; 2) the possible states of internal movement of bulk matter at room temperature cannot be represented as a (coherent) superposition of possibilities for Consciousness to choose from. This property is that decoherence.

So, although the micro-components of the macro remains quantum, due to decoherence, macroscopic matter such as our brain where we experience Consciousness does not normally offer a (coherent) superposition of possibilities for Consciousness to choose from.

Your materialist friend will at this point be triumphant: See what I have been telling you. Quantum physics does not apply to us, to the macroworld.

Revisit: How Consciousness connects to the macroworld. The answer is Experience and Software

How does Consciousness connect to macroscopic matter then? First let's discuss us, our brain. We never experience our brain without thought. I think; therefore, I am (identifying with my brain).

Thought is an experience of the mind, we say. The wisdom traditions somehow intuited that Consciousness connects to the physical (the brain) through what they called the subtle (in this case the mind) realm.

In the case of quantum measurement of an electron, we do know that we cannot measure the electron with our sense organs; we have to "see" it through a measurement aid apparatus, a three-dimensional grid of Geiger counters or a photographic plate, for example. Upon coupling to the quantum electron, a possibility object, the photographic plate becomes quantum, a possibility object as well.

Since mind is nonphysical (subtle) and moreover is quantum, then in a measurement situation, the brain acts as a measurement aid apparatus for the mind and acquires the quantum nature of the mind. In this way, Consciousness uses the intermediary of the quantum mind to connect to the brain as well as to give meaning to the sensory perception. Brain in its turn makes memory, including the thought as a correlated mental memory.

How Religions Compromise Spiritual Value Education

How are religions different from spiritual wisdom traditions? Religions are compromised forms of wisdom traditions, they introduce dogma. Religions propound elitism of a sort. Ordinary people cannot see the subtleties of consciousness, experiences, and the archetypal values; so some people, call them high priests, gurus, mullahs or by any other name—elitists all—in the name of giving people guidance, feed people dogma to manipulate them.

Religious education is a degenerated form of higher education that wisdom traditions initiated. It still dominates parts of our world. This form of education does teach the archetypes but obviously, the high priests, the teachers, they represent the authority of hearing the archetypal message; and they devise rituals for people to bring the archetypes in their life. The dogmas and rituals help to maintain the power of the authority over the masses.

Can there be free will and creativity in your effort to explore the archetypes if somebody has authority over you? In this way, the original intent of the idealist education is compromised in religious education.

Eventually, the religions managed to kill the idealist dogma-free creative spirit of education so much so that rebellion broke out within its ranks, a priest named Copernicus posthumously published an idea that led to a new way of thinking about reality. The rest is history.

The new way is of course science in its truth-seeking spirit, the science that, Newton, Darwin, Einstein, Freud, Jung, Heisenberg, and Maslow practiced. Its greatest virtue is that it is dogma free. It seeks the truth, no matter what the authority says. It gets its authority in a way that is almost fully above reproach, via verification and via application in technology. Somebody is proposing a theory, a map of the ideal of truth. You don't have to take that person's words for it, you check out the idea yourself in a way that not only can you but anybody else can also verify in principle. This way of combining the mental map-making of archetypes with experimental checks and balances defines modern truth-seeking science.

Since theory-making is always subject to the foibles of our meaning giving ordinary state of Consciousness, why could we not just use experiment to discern our experiences? Lots of people today want to take us back to this pure empiricism, evidence-based science. But as Albert Einstein, a great exponent of science in its true spirit said to another great scientist, Werner Heisenberg, empiricism without theory is a mirage. Implicitly as human beings, we always use mental models before we do anything. If we don't build theories explicitly, our theories will never go beyond primitive ideas. You can see ample evidence of this in evidence-based practice in today's health sciences—the experts incessantly arguing over evidence settling questions like: is coffee good for you?

The Materialists' Tactic: Deny Value-Education entirely

Up to the mid nineteen fifties, science, although enormously successful in some of its pursuits, was not getting anywhere with the questions of Consciousness and experience. The success story of science began only with Isaac Newton in the seventeenth century with his formulation of classical mechanics, how a system of mathematical equations based on physical laws can give us the power to calculate the movement of all material objects from falling apples to the stars and galaxies. Although many ideas have been added to what Newton theorized make the success of his basic theory more and more spectacular, all Newtonian science has always been a way to calculate the movement of objects. Our Consciousness, though, is one of a kind; it is both a subject and an object, an experiencer, conscious that it is separate in being from the experienced objects. It is capable of being conscious that it is categorically different yet embodied in an object. How can we ever make a science for the experiencing subject once we recognize our categorical difference from the objects of our experience?

For four hundred years, scientists had to put up with the religious models of the human side of things, and some of religion's seemingly absurd ideas, absurd when taken literally. Take the idea of God for example. In popular Christianity, God is a majestic king of kings, rules over everything. But scientists have been questioning that idea from the beginning: God does not rule over the behavior of matter, which is objective, independent of anyone, God's supposed omnipotence notwithstanding. Religions had to come to terms with that. But because of impotence of the Newtonian approach with the problem of human Consciousness and a few other things like how to distinguish between nonliving matter and living matter, scientists had to concede authority of what governs the human being to religion. A truce called the philosophy of modernism or Cartesian dualism, church with authority over how the human mind and Consciousness work, and science with the authority over the behavior of matter.

But there is a problem created by that old tendency of human beings that created religion, elitism in the pursuit of power. That call of elitism raised its head again. One way or another, the scientists of twentieth century got tired of sharing authority with religion. In the nineteen fifties, everything was going so well with scientific progress that nothing seemed to be unattainable for subjugation under the power of science.

A little technological advance is what however, broke the back of the proverbial camel, in this case Cartesian dualism or modernism. One of the vilest things religions did to most human cultures is to impose morality to curb one of our most natural conditioned drive—sexuality. Ok, this curb also had a natural deterrent, sex creates babies, wanted or unwanted. But suddenly, pharmaceutical research created the magic pill of birth control with 99% guarantee of success.

The fountain of sexuality broke out. The release of all that suppressed sexuality from the Victorian age onward now created a cultural change, an unprecedented avalanche of change. The elitism mongers among the scientists saw an opportunity to go with the flow of change and declared, we do not need to concede to religion the authority over mind and Consciousness. Let's declare! Science based on the everything-is-matter philosophy can give all answers.

But this is a dogma, you say. Yes, it is, nobody can prove that Consciousness, ideas, mental meaning, the vitality of feeling, are made of matter anymore than spiritual traditions and religions could prove that ideas are "real" like matter. So, a strategy developed: Make it an idealism versus realism debate. Collect circumstantial evidence in favor of the material metaphysics, and create doubt about all the evidence against such a dogma crying pseudoscience (since science is now defined as only realist thinking possible, science within the primacy of matter) then argue, What else can reality be since ideas are not real? And admonish the opponents, Get real.

This seems like a winning tactic! To label your opponents the way they should label you! Science with dogma *is* pseudoscience. Trump did that a lot. All the news media that tried calling his lies, he called fake news!

Can anybody deny that we cannot detect with our apparatuses any of these nonphysical things that the philosophy of idealism proposes? Yeah, some people say that they can experience them, but not without our brain, without matter! Yes, the living seems to behave differently than the nonliving, they seem to have purpose. In the analogy of the computer, yes while matter is only hardware, living matter seems to have living software with its own laws of vitalism. Yet, who can deny that life does not exist without material body. This makes it ok to declare that living software is also created by matter, it is an emergent epiphenomenon, secondary phenomenon, of matter.

Suppose all conscious experiences are just ornamental epiphenomenon of the complexity of the brain! Suppose life, meaning, values, all are epiphenomena of the complexity of material organization!

Science based on primacy of matter will explain it all, there is no need to suffer from religion and its moral impositions on human nature, is there?

How Scientific Materialists Try to De-Construct Idealism and Idealist Education: the Details

1. DENY CONSCIOUSNESS

If education is removal of ignorance to enable people to "see" things better, we are assuming that people are conscious. There is "somebody" in there, in that brain behind the eyes to understand things in his or her own way. But it may be just a "ghost" we invent. Isn't it more scientific to posit instead that Consciousness is just a ghost in the machine, that we are indeed just the brain, material machines, much like those silicon computers but made of carbon?

These promoters of scientific materialism and machine view of us forcefully point out that their way is objective. How can we do science without strict objectivity? Should not all our social systems be guided by an objective science and be independent of somebody's whims and idiosyncratic thinking?

Puzzled already? How does one refute such solid arguments?

2. DENY MEANING GIVING MIND

If light shines in a room, then if we are conscious and can cognize the meaning of what is happening, we see better. But who needs to conclude that this needs the assumption of a nonphysical mind? Yes, brain is a computer, but suppose it is not bound by the limitations of the silicon computer! The brain makes its own software, call it mind if you wish, to give meaning to material stimuli; in other words, the brain is a cognizing computer.

3. DENY FREE WILL AND CREATIVITY

Do we have to assume that people can opt to gather knowledge and change their ways of ignorant lifestyle, when so much evidence says otherwise—that people do not really change; they are perfectly happy to remain where they are?

Scientific materialists also say this. We do not have free will; what we have is the illusion of free will. And additionally, being machines, we operate on the software we are born with; some additional software we create trying to survive and adapt to ambient environmental changes during our formative period. And education is about this latter part. Information and job training that is what our survival demands. And by the way, *I, we, you* are just operational words to speak of the brain.

Face it, declares the new priests of scientific materialism. We have debunked idealism. Our ideas are no more than fingers pointing to the moon that does not exist. Our relationship with everyone else in our environment is transactional; that is what machines do. All we need is information for carrying out transaction. The world is not made of Consciousness, it is made of information.

4. DENY HIERARCHY OF NEEDS AND THE ARCHETYPES TO SATISFY THEM

Archetypes are debunked as ideas pointing to a phantom reality that cannot be verified, let them go. Do we have to assume that we have need beyond our survival needs? Yes, we talk about love, but could it not be a euphoric effect of the sex hormone of oxytocin? And similarly, do you not see that your value related emotions are the results of similar other molecules of emotions, dopamine, endorphin, etc.?

So here is the crunch. The proponents of the removal of ignorance view of education are tacitly assuming that knowledge consists not only of knowledge that we see with our eyes—the material world—but also what we don't see with our eyes—ideas.

Whom do you trust? People who base their thinking about education with what we can see, what we can objectively develop into a science based on matter that everybody can see and build the consensus (science) or education based on airy fairy ideas?

To summarize: all this kind of challenge creates a lot of ambiguities in people's mind; add to this the promise of unlimited worldly goodies. Thus was how entire countries and cultures bought into the transactional valueless education that prevails now. The religionists opposed of course; but they had nothing better to offer; their dogmas, taken literally, go against empirical evidence and are often even worse for elevating the human condition.

The Idealists' Quantum Response: *See for yourself that Materialist Science is an unscientific pseudoscience*

What is education ultimately is a debate on how we see ourselves, a debate about our worldview. It has always been that way except until about 1960, the idealists had prevailed to some extent; there was a truce between science and religion. In the last six decades though, education has changed from the previous view of removal of ignorance to information and job training because unnoticed by the society at large, a majority of academics in the USA and Europe, prompted by the success of scientists who study matter and adopt materialism as a convenient tool of domination over the competition—religion, adopted a highly partisan and unscientific worldview falsely called scientific materialism—materialism with science backing it.

Why is this way of doing science unscientific? Science by definition isa knowledge system we develop to the cause of finding the truth about everything—*it is about removal of ignorance.* It is that fundamental ideal—the soul of science—that the materialist scientists are trying to destroy. Science does not make materialism scientific. Instead, if science wears a materialist garb, it becomes a science with dogma—pseudoscience by definition.

As to the claim of strict objectivity, it is a false claim! The study of radioactivity reveals that radioactive decay is not strictly replicable; the replication is only on the average. In this way, quantum mechanics only has room for a weak objectivity. Experimental data need not be independent of observers; all it needs is to be essentially same according to those who can see.

To reemphasize: Materialist science is a pseudoscience masquerading as science. Its promissory philosophy of epiphenomenalism is not a verifiable philosophy, it is not a scientific theory!

Hush hush, close the doors, this is heresy against today's scientific orthodoxy. But do not worry. Materialist science has succeeded in its power play with spiritual traditions and religion but only partway. Several things keep people from making total commitment to it.

One is simple politics. Democracy as practiced in the USA supports two-party politics. When one party sides with dogmatic science, it is advantageous for the other party to gravitate toward dogmatic religion to rile up support. This political battle is going on in many countries and cultures today: USA, Brazil, India, Israel, Iran just to name a few.

The other factor is Exclusion. Dogma excludes; it negates a lot of people's living experience. People who feel excluded look for alternatives.

Debate Continues: How Science Within Materialism Loses its Credibility

Materialist science accepted the dogma of materialism at its own peril. It may coopt intellectuals by the allure of elitist power, vast segments of ordinary people are not fooled by it. Instead, they lose faith in science.

When I (Amit) was a physics professor and a materialist at that, there was no scientific alternative those days, I was constantly puzzled by the anti-science attitude of nonscience students. Those young people just did not trust the scientific ways. I did not know why, not then. Now I know. They could see that materialist science does not support arts and the humanities, which is what they liked, what they were actively pursuing for a career. They felt threatened, they felt excluded.

Moreover, dogmatic materialist science, trying to get rid of the archetypes, also, gets rid of the archetype of truth. How would they argue around that and justify validity for the laws of science? Materialists say, Just as brain develops its mental software, so do elementary particles of matter develop their "laws of physics" via the complexity of the random motion of a substratum of the elementary particles. Such ideas have been tried but have not gotten any traction among even materialist scientists! But nevertheless, the belief continues implicitly.

That the brain is a cognizing computing machine is a prime example of the implicit promissory materialism passed as gospel truth.

It all comes back to political correctness. The liberals insist that it is not politically correct to oppose materialist science—warts or not.

The net effect of all this pretension is chaos. Witness the decline of civilization going on in the USA right now. And in quite a few other countries as well.

What the Materialist Model of Education Assumes and what Materialists Try to Hide

Let's begin our discussion with the two prongs of materialist education that students receive in our secular public schools and colleges as well as those private institutions that go along with secularism. These prongs I have already mentioned: information processing and job training.

There is one other implicit understanding: human being is a transactional behavioral being made of matter: whatever universal software it carries originated as epiphenomena of material interaction during the roughly four billion years of biological evolution from one-celled organisms to the human organism out of the Darwinian mechanisms of chance mutation of genes and survival necessity of adapting to environmental changes. The universal software gives us those negative emotional brain circuits as well as circuits of pleasure that enable us the four F-responses: fleeing, fighting, f-king, and feeding. This defines the role of nature in human development. Additionally, responding to environmental stimuli during our formative years, humans develop individual brain software of "nurture."

In this way, there is a corollary, another implicit assumption: we are what we are; the software and hardware, both being the result of the laws of physics are beyond our control. We can do some genetic engineering to alter some of the circuits, but that is about it.

Educators in our schools, colleges, and universities have willfully submitted to wearing this straightjacket. The word straightjacket was used by one of the architects of materialist science—physicist Richard Feynman—trying to explain to a bunch of budding scientists why they must wear the straightjacket of scientific materialism. Most of these educators, if not all, realize that the old-fashioned archetypal values are important for both the human self and their societies; and yet they play with ideas for concealment, they dance with words of sophistry, pretending that meaning processing is still possible, even Consciousness and feelings may emerge from material evolution because they have survival value. So, some philosophers get busy trying to prove that with endless ideas of more skillful words of sophistry.

Other thinkers admit it only when under opponents' pressure! Yes, they are assuming that there is no scientific validity for human values; values are human made. Civilization seems to need some of these values just as it needs criminal laws. So,

1. we will pretend to have these values, a philosophy of political correctness of our speech is supremely important.

2. The chaos from value ambiguity must be taken care of by legalizing values and following strict law and order.

Or so they hope. Any which way to save the dogma of materialism—all is matter—and the pleasureful lifestyle and permissive society it guarantees.

Religions have done the same thing in the past. Religions knew they are polluting the concept of the archetypes by introducing religious dogma and undermining the spirit of all science, not just materialist science; what else can they do to keep people under their leash except to support their own dogmas and spread conspiracy theories? Transformation? Out of the question.

Behold! On one hand, the two sets of dogma have created conceptual chaos and today's dangerous divisive power politics that both sides seem to play; on the other hand, if the religious side did not keep the pressure on, it is hard to imagine the evils of archetypal denial and amorality, the kind of permissive society that materialists without opposition would have created.

Seeing for Yourself

In the final reckoning you have to see for yourself the validity of your consciousness, all your experiences, of archetypes and of creativity and transformation. A very short list as a preparation for the rest of the book.

1. *Consciousness*: try to discover your "I" behind your "me". Meditation can help. Hint: occasionally you will find yourself relaxed, happy. Your consciousness has expanded with the experience of "I"–**your quantum self.**

2. *Experiences*. Experience ambiguity, metaphors. Read mythology. Do not buy into other people's meaning without questioning them and this includes the present authors.

Delve into feeling in the body. Discover the chakras as centers of feeling. Practice chi gong, pranayama, yoga; these practices will experientially revel that what you feel is vital energy. It is real.

Engage in creativity. Alternative imaginative thinking and relaxing while still retaining some focus on the creative question you are exploring. A process we call do-be-do-be-do. Enjoy the occasional insights this brings, not big bangs necessarily, but little bangs to be sure.

3. *Get into archetypes.* Love for example. Try to discover the quantum brain and the quantum heart beyond the way you experience your brain and heart now.

PART 2

Hero's Journey: Transformational Education Requires Transformed Teachers—Heroes

Quantum Education: Initiation into Hero's Journey—Challenging Your Belief System and Changing it

In the olden days of consciousness research millennia ago, all participants and would-be-teachers had a one-pointed goal—self-realization. This was their dharma. For self-realized teachers there was only one way of removing ignorance in those days, only one archetype to explore creatively for transformation. The creative process was not known, however; one had to follow the great teachers' path, and most times, those paths took one only partway. So eventually, the seeker had to chart his or her own path. The whole process took a considerable amount of time.

Self-realization in those days mostly used the intellect and the creative insight came in the form of an enlightening wisdom specific to the seeker whose ultimate message was the idealist metaphysics: consciousness is the ground of all being. This intellectual exploration was later called the wisdom path—jnana (pronounced gnyana in Sanskrit with a nasal hard g sound) Yoga.

Today, quantum science has made it easy. Jnana yoga is not needed. Instead, you can follow science's method for finding truth: theory and experiment instead of theory and experience. Saves you a considerable amount of time.

The dharma for professionals other than teachers depended on the profession: the warriors pursued the archetype of power, businesspeople the archetype of abundance, artists the archetype of beauty, and so forth.

All this changes in quantum science. Ignorance is not defined solely by the ignorance of the true nature of the self. Ignorance is mistaking the self as me—an object—and forget the subject "I" that is behind the me. Also, ignorance that the "I" can be temporarily expanded to include the you-other to make a "we." Caring for the other expands our self-perception to include not only relationships of intimacy but also to the community. This not recognizing the community-self is behind the societal and environmental crisis today.

Quantum science and empirical data seem to suggest a chronological order of archetypal exploration that a transformation-seeker can engage. The step-by-step process makes it much easier to gauge success and maintain motivation.

For the educationist, the teacher, the final goal is wholeness; however, one can work on wholeness while exploring the earlier archetypes in the chronology revealed by the data.

The first step is to straighten out how to think, how to straighten out all worldview confusion. This takes a considerable belief system re-visioning.

In earlier chapters, we have touched upon the basics of quantum physics and quantum science as well as the quantum worldview. In this chapter let's start with some verifying data.

Starting with the nineteen eighties new data started coming in challenging the basic tenets of scientific materialism; at the same time, maverick theoretical scientists started to explore alternative avenues fora paradigm shift in science.

The new data and new ideas are now coming in profusely in support of the quantum science paradigm from everywhere: physics, biology, neuroscience, psychology, even computer science, what have you. We will give you a list:

- *Quantum physics*: An experiment by a group of physicists headed by Alain Aspect has demonstrated a phenomenon called non-locality: signal-less communication.

- *Quantum physics and quantum measurement theory*: Using an approximation to the quantum equation, the physicist David Bohm mathematically demonstrated the existence of a domain of reality (implicate order) outside of space and time (explicate order). Systems theorist Ervin Laszlo saw the quantum domain of potentiality as a nonlocal quantum field. Amit Goswami generalized earlier ideas of von Neumann and showed that the quantum field is nothing but consciousness and it is the ground of being of not only material possibilities but also quantum possibilities of our experiences of meaning, feeling, and intuition. Science within consciousness was born with the explanation of how consciousness creates the material world via downward causation.

- *Psychology*: the phenomenon of blindsight—a cortically blind person is found to avoid an obstacle on his way while walking but denies that he saw the obstacle—was observed in 1969 and confirmed Freud's old idea of the unconscious once dismissed as voodoo psychology. Quantum science is able to explain the science behind the unconscious: it is the unmanifest quantum domain of potentiality. In other words, unconscious is consciousness without awareness, without subject-object split.

- *Neuroscience*: A whole bunch of neuroscience experiments have demonstrated that electrical activity can be nonlocally (without electrical signals) can be transferred from one brain in meditative connection with another. This is called transferred potential. The first such demonstration was due to the neuroscientist Jacobo Grinberg-Zylberbaum and collaborators. The experiment verified that the brains of two observers can be correlated and the correlation can be maintained if the observers meditate with the intention for nonlocal communication.

- Biology: How to differentiate life from nonlife? This sentience—the ability to experience the world as conscious subject—is then the property that differentiates between life and nonlife.

What is feeling? Biologists have known for a long time that even single cell creatures have feeling, they feel their way about their environment. Harold Baxter demonstrated that plants can feel pain.

We have the living world without the cortical brain, from a single living cell to mammals below the primates in the evolutionary totem pole.

Instead of the mind, these living beings without the neo-cortex connect to Consciousness via the vital—one of the organizing principles of life. We experience the movement of the vital software as feeling.

- *Biology*: While trying to find explanation for cell differentiation—why cells in different organs make different sets of proteins even though all cells possess identical genes—Rupert Sheldrake discovered nonmaterial morphogenetic fields. Materialist scientists threatened to burn Sheldrake's book; the controversy was dualism implicit in Sheldrakes theory. Goswami incorporated Sheldrake's discovery in the science within consciousness resolving the controversy.

Human fetus begins as a one cell embryo called zygote. All our organs are built from that one cell becoming many by cell division. In this way all cells have the same genes. Then how are they differentiated so cells in different organs activate different sets of genes to make proteins appropriate for the functioning of the organ to which it belongs? Different software you say. Ok. The plot thickens with mystery however, when you realize that often organs in different parts of the body act in instant coordination suggesting signal-less communication. Material local interactions cannot simulate nonlocality, so we need a nonphysical quantum field to help Consciousness organize the organ software. This nonmaterial quantum field is what Sheldrake called morphogenetic field.

- *Biology*: A series of experiments in biology has verified Sheldrake's idea that the operating software of biological organs is epigenetic; the prefix epi means outside.

- *Physiology*: The result of repeated experiences of feeling of the vital movements of the morphogenetic fields along with the sensing of the organ physiology gives us the vital software that turns on organ physiology.

- *Yoga Psychology*: The experience of organ physiology together with vital software occurs at points of the body roughly along the spine. These points are called the chakras first discovered in yoga psychology millennia ago. Amit Goswami ha discovered the quantum science of the chakras.

- *Biophysics*: A new technique called Kirlian photography has demonstrated that not only do we have a bioelectric layer on our skin but also the field of this layer is sensitive to our feelings in this way providing a way of measuring feelings.

- *Directed mutation*: The biologist John Cairns and his collaborators discovered that a colony of simple bacterium, when proffered lactose that they cannot digest, hasten up their mutation rate for mutation into another species that can digest lactose. They aptly called the process directed mutation. Obviously, the experiment verifies the idea of downward causation by consciousness.

- *Neuroscience*: Experiments of neuroscience via the technique of magnetic resonance imaging (MRI) have demonstrated that brain states imaged are sensitive to mental states people simultaneously experience. In other words, mental experience, mind, is measurable.

- *Neuroscience*: Experiments on neuroscience based on the new technology called functional magnetic resonance imaging (fMRI) has revealed that our brain can operate in two modalities: local (centered around being that communicates with signal and nonlocal centered around being that communicates without signals and therefore involves many distant parts of the brain simultaneously.

- *Neuroscience*: The brains of people in acts of intelligence show more synaptic connections among different parts suggesting nonlocality and expansion of consciousness.

- *Quantum physics*: The quantum physicist Niels Bohr theorized that when electrons jump from one atomic orbit to another, they do not go through the intervening space. This is called a quantum leap. Recently, it has been verified that when electrons traverse across an energy barrier in a transistor, they do not tunnel through as previously theorized. Instead, the new measurements confirmed the quantum leap theory.

- *Creativity Research*: Decades of case studies by creativity researchers have revealed that creative insights come to people discontinuously. Amit Goswami explained the discontinuity of creative experiences as quantum leaps of meaningful thoughts leading to new meaning.

- *Biological Evolution*: biologists have discovered fossil gaps of evolution—the fossil data is not continuous and consequently nor is evolution, as once thought, as in Darwin's theory. The biologists Niles Eldredge and Stephen Gould proposed the theory of punctuated equilibrium—evolution in addition to continuous prose of Darwinian vintage occasionally display abrupt punctuation marks. Amit Goswami has demonstrated the gaps—punctuation marks of evolution—consists of quantum leaps of creativity.

- *Health science*: many cases of spontaneous healing without any medical intervention were discovered. The physician Deepak Chopra identified them as a demonstration of discontinuous quantum healing—quantum leaps of healing.

- *Neuroscience*: the neuroscientist Mario Bureaugard has demonstrated that when Carmelite nuns have out-of-the-body experiences, there is a neural correlate that tells us exactly that, their brain center of body awareness—the parietal lobe—goes numb, in this way validating the phenomenon of out-of-the-body experience much touted in the spiritual literature.

- *Parapsychology*: Distant viewing experiments—one psychic sees an object in a town square and makes a mental image; another psychic is able to draw a picture of the object while sitting in a closet at a distance obviously without any local signals from the other. This confirms the much-touted phenomenon of mental telepathy. Quantum science provides an explanation: the two psychics are correlated via intention of direct communication. For correlated electrons, the correlation breaks up as soon as we measure. In the case of humans, the psychics maintain the correlation by ongoing meditative intention on direct communication.

- *Health science*: Healing at a distance has been demonstrated by the physician Randolph Byrd; people pray for the healing of patients in Denver; this hastens up the patients' recovery from cardiac surgery in San Francisco.

- *Artificial Intelligence theory*: the philosopher John Searle theorized that computers cannot process meaning; this was verified via mathematics by the physicist Roger Penrose. If the brain works like a computer as it seems to, then it follows that the brain cannot cognize.

- *Cognitive science*: the cognitive scientist Tony Marcel demonstrated that processing ambiguous words with or without conscious awareness affect people's cognition time. If the brain could cognize, it would make no difference whether people are consciously aware of an event or not. Conclusion: brain cannot cognize.

- *Reincarnation*: This is a very old idea that originated in India. Some essence of us somehow continues after our death and transmigrates to an aborning baby in some future time and place; in other words, in some sense we survive the death of our current physical body and reincarnate into another physical body in the future. This theory was languishing as an evocative idea and nothing more, although from time to time there were strange stories of little children recalling incidents from their past lives. In the twentieth century, the psychiatrist Ian Stevenson took the idea seriously and established definitive data that what these children described really happened. Amit Goswami has theoretically explained this phenomenon with the concept of nonlocal memory of learning. The brain researcher Karl Lashley has demonstrated the validity of the concept of nonlocal of learning.

- *Jungian Psychology of Collective unconscious.* Jung discovered that in some evocative big dreams, we all have the experience of remembering shared memory, we see universal symbols that triggers in us the same evocative archetypal resonance. Dreams of angels, gods and goddesses fall in this category. To explain the data, Jung theorized that the symbols are a part of humanity's collective unconscious; Amit Goswami further theorized that the symbols are representations of the Platonic archetypes and explained how our ancestors could be nonlocally connected while they underwent archetypal transformation to make collective nonlocal memory. We will call these representations Jungian archetypes for future reference.

- *Synchronicity*: another great theoretical idea from Jung. They are incidences of the occurrence of a physical event simultaneously and coincidentally with somebody's mental revelation of meaning. In other words, synchronicities are examples of meaningful coincidences between something physical and something mental. You must wonder: are they due to a common cause? Quantum science says yes. The common cause is nonlocal Consciousness. We cannot verify synchronicity via laboratory experiments. But if you are open to them, you will easily find plenty of experiential confirmation of the idea.

- *Inner Creativity: Hero's Journey.* The mythologist Joseph Campbell discovered the myth of the hero's journey as a universal journey of inner creativity and transformation. Carl Jung discovered the details.

We could go on and on, but you get the picture. Experimental data is so important to convince yourself of a new idea. Take the case of vital energy. It is the movement associated with feeling; it feels like energy. If we call it *vital energy* who can object? But when we say it is nonphysical, you hesitate if you have a belief that all energy is physical, all energy is related to movement of matter. But when you examine a Kirlian photograph of your finger tip and can see for yourself how the photograph changes as your mood changes and you cannot explain this in any purely physical way, like moisture on your finger, people tried you know, then you are more prone to admit what Hamlet said to Horatio: there are more things in heaven and earth than are dreamt of in your philosophy.

Or take the case of nonlocality. For decades the parapsychology experiments have always been debunked by the "skeptical inquirers" for one reason or another, mostly because a little subjectivity is always involved. But when you see the data on transferred potential and see the similarity of EEG readings of the brain waves of two guys, one sitting in an electrically impervious Faraday chamber, and yet only the other guy has seen light flashes, you do a double take (fig. 4a). Electrical activity can be transferred from one brain to another simply because the two people are continuously meditating with the intention of direct nonlocal communication during the experiment? Unbelievable! But look, when the two subjects do not meditate (control subjects), there is no transferred potential (3b)

What is experimental proof? Long time ago, it was seeing is believing. Copernicus and instrumentation changed all that. Instruments can amplify and this expands our ability of seeing. But then came the idea of quark; you cannot see it even with an electron microscope because it is always confined; it never sees daylight. The mindset had to change before they gave a Nobel prize to the physicist who led the group who did the crucial experiment that established the existence of quark via an indirect measurement, because there was no other explanation. This change in mindset is enabling us to develop data for quantum science within consciousness.

And now the most welcome news for all educationists of idealist values: notice this !*one scientific theory called quantum science has been able to integrate all the alternative avenues of recent times alluded to above under one umbrella. This is the most convincing piece of data.* Coincidentally, this new science, also completely validates the philosophy of idealism that the ancient seers discovered via experience.

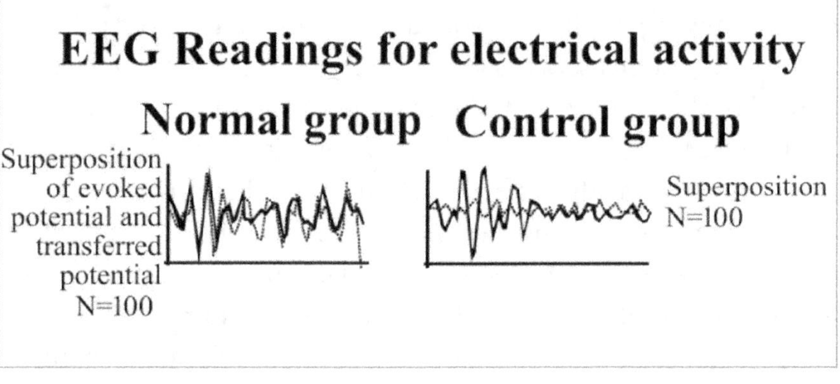

Figure 4. Transferred potential. When people are nonlocal correlated via continuous meditative intention electric potential is transferred from one brain to another, this is show in left. For the control group, no correlation between the subjects, no transferred potential is found.

Yes, quantum physics gives us quantum science based on a genuine scientific and monistic metaphysics of idealism, no less. It is not a false claim of monism like scientific materialism. It has no dogma;

it is not a pseudoscience like materialist science. This time, the use of the word scientific is legit; quantum science has no dogma, its metaphysics is verifiable and verified. The seemingly metaphysical idea of Oneness of Consciousness is a fully verified scientific notion of nonlocal Consciousness; if you call it metaphysics, the metaphysics is experimental metaphysics, a term coined by the physicist Abner Shimony.

Once you take a mini quantum leap to the understanding of the worldview of Scientific quantum idealism, you can rest assured that it will give you all the right thinking for you to re-vision and restructure your current belief system, making it easy to live and engage in your profession—including educating students—in synchrony with your thinking.

Dealing with the Undeniable Base-level Human Condition

If in this life in today's culture, you are thinking of choosing the education profession, there is little doubt that you have some reincarnational maturity under your belt. Even so with the current myopia of parenting, caregivers, and teachers, one cannot avoid developing some tendencies characterizing the base-level condition:

- Me-centeredness. This will tend to make your adult relationships transactional, what is in it for me?

- Your brain, the midbrain to be specific, is still loaded with negative emotional brain circuits, of violence and domination, of hatred and jealousy, of lust and competitiveness. This means, you, too, suffer from the conditioning of being more negative than positive.

- Your brain will also have pleasure circuits and you will have to deal with pleasure-seeking tendencies—such as looking at people as pleasure-objects—as well.

- With all the information technology available today, the tendency to maintain status quo combined with the tendency to avoid boredom, leads to the habit of processing much more information than ever before (as in slavery to checking the cell phone). You will have to deal with that tendency, too.

These tendencies will make barriers against your creative explorations. But there is some saving grace coming your way as well.

What is a human being in the base-level condition ignorant of? It is the completely oblivion that there are infinite potentialities to manifest and change for the better. In this base-level condition people cannot process the idea that change is possible, that transformation can and does happens if we explore the possibilities. If other people claim they have changed, the base-level people react like, "I am faking it, so they must be faking it." Ignorance does that to you.

And yet, since you are not in this base level condition, you have creativity and you already have engaged for outer accomplishments. In other words, you recognize and respond to higher needs to some degree. You can easily see that there isa substantial number of people around you who likewise have discovered higher needs; some of them even explore the archetypes with inner creativity and create shining example of what can be achieved if you explore your human potentialities with transformation in mind!

There have been transformed people in the past, too. They have always told people about human potentialities, but distractors have always been able to sabotage their teachings. Look at the history of human civilization: it is full of ups and down. Up when wisdom prevails and there is some transformational education, and down is when the saboteurs succeed.

Today, many people feel hopeless because they can see that both the lenses we use today—religion and science—are dogmatic, exclusive, and therefore divisive. They also see that the proponents of both worldviews are hypocrites. They lose their faith in both religion and science. They despair. The culture is a culture of either avoidance or despair.

The way back to hope is the first important step to take. Suspend your disbelief and despair. If you are reading this book, you are already searching for hope. If you have absorbed the lessons of the previous chapters, you also realize this: religion is not spirituality, and materialist science with dogma is not true science.

Behold! The truth-seeking quantum theorists—Einstein, Bohr, Heisenberg, Schrödinger, von Neuman, Eugene Wigner, Fred Alan Wolf, John Bell, David Bohm, Alain Aspect, John Wheeler, Nick Herbert, Henry Stapp, and many others including Amit—never stopped their struggle with understanding the message of quantum physics, what is it that it is trying to tell us. These efforts did not succeed in time to arrest the advent of materialist science, but they are having an effect now.

Hope: Paradigm Shift in Science is giving you an Option to Straighten up your Worldview towards Hope

A genuine possibility of a paradigm shift from a matter-based science to a consciousness-based science has arisen in physics and science. It has no discernible effect on the hard sciences and engineering/technology. So, don't be surprised with denials from those quarters even though their denial gets a lot of media support.

Just notice that soft sciences are already responding. There is talk—small voices no doubt—of quantum biology from biologists like Bruce Lipton. In health sciences, Deepak Chopra and Larry Dossey have popularized the concepts of quantum leaps and quantum nonlocality. In psychology, thanks to Carl Jung, Abraham Maslow, Stan Grof, James Hillman, Haridas Choudhury, and Roberto Assagioli, transpersonal and depth psychologies are strong forces. In systems theory, the great Ervin Laszlo has given us the concept of quantum field.

The new science paradigm, the quantum science of Consciousness is based on quantum physics, however; its concepts are foreign to specialists of soft sciences. Don't expect soft scientists and philosophers to invest in and learn these concepts any time soon either.

In the nineties, when I (Amit) had an inkling of the scope of the new paradigm, how it may be able to find a bridge between all the new paradigm thinking that was going on at the time with a renowned transpersonal psychologist, Roger Walsh. I was lamenting and complaining about the attitude of benign neglect toward my work even from transpersonal psychologists who base their psychology on the primacy of Consciousness. "Roger, it just does not make sense. Look, quantum physics is giving the scientific basis for transpersonal psychology." The wise Roger just smiled. "Be patient. It takes time."

A few days later, one of the founders of transpersonal psychology, Stan Grof called me and congratulated me for the publication of *The Self-Aware Universe.* In the year 1996, the celebrated exponent of transpersonal psychology in Brazil, Pierre Weil, understood the power of the quantum paradigm so much that he incorporated it in his model of transformational education in Brazil. I taught in his organization of *Unipaz* for quite a while.

In 2000, I was a keynote speaker at the European conference on Transpersonal Psychology. When I met Roger there, he smiled and said with a wink. "See what I told you."

Change: The Quantum Spark

So, there is hope. When the meaning of quantum physics becomes clear, to our surprise we discover that we have a science of consciousness in our hand; we have a science of the human experience, how we can be an object as well as a subject embedded in a physical body.

And the surprise of surprises is that the consciousness we have discovered in science, the consciousness that quantum measurement theory introduces, is the same Oneness-consciousness that the founders of the spiritual wisdom traditions discovered via direct experience. When you realize that the wisdom traditions have left us a treasure-trove of transformative techniques and practices which now quantum science is explaining and optimizing, you will be filled with hope.

Finally, there is now a clear bridge between reality as is it is and the human condition. Anyone can walk the bridge and reach the heights of wisdom. Finally, know that there is a science of transformation, and we are developing it further.

We will tell you more about the bridge and the journey (hero's journey) needed to scale it (yes, scaling is the correct word, because the bridge is really a ladder going to new heights of human consciousness) in the next chapter.

The saving Grace of the current higher education is that at least we have not lost the archetypes entirely. We still talk about the jobs that we prepare for in terms of professions. Unbeknownst to the materialist, these professions were created for the exploration of archetypes and some people still choose their profession from an intuitive attraction they feel toward it (the archetype attractor principle). Science is the exploration of the archetype of Truth, the fine arts are an exploration of the archetype of beauty, business, and economics of the archetype of abundance, politics is for the archetype of power, law serves the archetype of justice, religious counselling serves the archetype of goodness and love, psychology, medicine and education are about the archetype of wholeness.

It is the poverty of materialist survival thinking that have denigrated these professions and made them into jobs that you do for businesses and corporations, the government, and churches, and so called higher educational institutions. What is taught, likewise, are about how to make your job sound complex enough for your employers and the products you make attractive enough for your consumers.

The knowledge you pick up at the institutions of higher education prepare you for the job which is tailor made for the education you receive; that's the whole idea right? It earns you a living, a lot of money, a lot of power to dominate others. And yet, after a current while, you discover, it is not satisfying. Satisfying what? Your survival needs have been long satisfied! Reluctantly, you recognize an old word that you thought is to be thrown away, you thought it is not scientific. But it describes your situation perfectly! So, you admit to yourself: my job is not satisfying my *soul*. Ponder over what that thought may be indicating. You have a soul.

Do You have a Soul or Is It just Wishful Thinking?

Yes, Virginia, yes, Adriano, or whatever your name is, if you are interested in becoming a quantum educator, you already have a soul to some degree. How? And why and how did it get so obscure even to you?

Parental and teacher care today have much wrongness The current theories of child development and social mores on which they are based ignore several important aspects of being human:

1. Spirit is embodied in human beings, that children are born as a spiritual quantum self.

2. Babies are nonlocally correlated with their mother while in the womb and that correlation continues even as the baby separates from the mother. In other words, nonlocal communication at least at the vital level remains strong between mother and child for quite a while in the early years.

3. It takes over a period of about five years to achieve the differentiation and separateness of the regular consciousness in children that we call the beginning of a mental ego associated with the brain-mind.

4. Young children have both vital feelings and mental thinking capacities; there are universal built-in software for

both in humanity's collective unconscious. The child from age 0 to 5 adds to the universal software personal software by its living and thinking dynamics.

5. The first year of child development is almost exclusively development of personal vital software; age 1 through 5, both mental and vital.

6. Because of the very active presence of the quantum self, children do get intuition, but they lack the fully formed representational apparatus until about age 5, but again more in the mental than in the vital. So, this is a murky area but don't forget reincarnation and the phenomenon of talent. In any case, children in general are aware about intuitions; and they do represent it in feeling and have feelings at the navel, and the heart chakra.

7. Both mother's love and other love enable most children to take mini quantum leaps of awakening at the heart chakra; they develop an altruistic software, and a self at the heart for using it.

8. The developmental psychologist Eric Ericson has theorized based on his experience with children that children develop autonomy between age five and seven when they shift their attention from parents to their pier group. The autonomy is a signature of the awakening of the navel chakra: I am responsible for my own security; I can make my own decisions and take responsibility for it.

9. After they learn the three R's, children, at least the talented and gifted ones, are ready to learn abstract thinking, understanding, and processing personal meaning out of other people's meaning. Since children of this young age are still strong at intuitions, they take mini quantum leaps for this purpose. In this way, their ego, too, becomes 'woke' of intuitive thought and develop soul software of a higher mind.

10. At about age 14, many youngsters have further awakening of the navel chakra (while developing the notion of meaning and purpose of their lives) and of the heart chakra (while exploring romantic love).

In this way, it is clear that as children many people do develop a soul although the current information-based rational culture prevents many children from doing so as well. Unfortunately, even for those who develop a soul, there are brain-mind doshas—excessive inertia, hyperactivity, and intellectualism (a tendency to use the rational rather than intuition) that develop and cover the soul as clouds cover the sun.

Recovering the Soul and re-Visioning Jobs into Satisfying Professions

Transformational education using quantum science is a program 1) to "recover your soul," and when that is accomplished, 2) to engage in further soul-making. So, with quantum education, as you recover your soul and engage in further soul-making, you also rediscover the soul of your profession as well.

Quantum science integrates and incorporates all the truth other explorers have discovered previously albeit using the wrong context. And guess what! Machines are complex, the hard science of our hardware is complex. But the software is not. A human being does not have to be complex or learn complex things to be healthy, prosperous, and happy.

All these fields—health sciences, economics and business, education and psychology—when illuminated by the right wisdom indeed become simple. Why should be any different? They are just the vehicles for the human "search of the soul."

When you glimpse your soul, glimpse it with new quantum concepts, quantum education teaches you how to live those concepts, how to feel them in your being, how to make the soul learning alive in you.

When you engage your profession so educated with wisdom, having integrated thinking, and feeling, you earn your livelihood in synchrony with how you think and how you live. This is what satisfies your soul.

By changing the ways of your profession, you will be changing the world as well; please see it and feel the inspiration from it. When all professionals change their me centered ways to soul development, the world becomes endowed with a soul, too. The great psychologist Carl Jung called this the world soul. The visionary Teilhard the Chardin saw it as heaven on earth, the awakened philosopher Sri Aurobindo saw it as the awakening of Supramental Intelligence. Quantum physics sees it as the embodiment of wholeness.

This is the goal of transformative education—quantum style. Quantum science does not disappoint. It gives us both ontology—the science of our being, and epistemology—how to scale the ladder that takes us to higher and higher beings. It is a soul satisfying adventure.

Transformational Education—Quantum Style

Liberal education, even the old-fashioned dogma-free kind, has always emphasized mental education; even our creativity, by and large is mental creativity, even with free reigns on exploring archetypes, they were mental exploration through the ages.

To get out of the shackles of the human condition we need transformational education, education that will transform the human condition into more positive stations of homeostasis; and that means, stations of more health, more prosperity, more happiness. This we accomplish by not only learning the quantum worldview—who we are and what our relationship is with our environment—but also applying the knowledge learned to live our life accordingly. And more. Changing the society and its systems so that we can make a living without compromising our worldview and the modus of our living. In this way, transformative education consists of the following interdependent tracks:

1. Learning how to think; otherwise, worldview;

2. Learning how-to live-in congruence with and using the quantum worldview; this involves some intellectual but mostly experiential practice and creativity-oriented education;

3. Learn how to scale the ladder of happiness from neurosis to normal to positive to enlightened states of soul-being (see chapter 8);

4. Learning the quantum science's way of how our social systems should work. This means learning quantum science of health and healing, quantum science of building prosperity for ourselves and for our society, and the quantum science of child development, and the quantum science of happiness. The quantum science of prosperity involves many facets: the quantum science of economics, business administration, and business entrepreneurship, the quantum science of politics, the quantum science of ethics and morality, the quantum science of social justice.

5. Learn how to engage in a profession in the quantum way;

6. Learn how to lead the rest of the society toward quantum thinking, living, and earning livelihood;

7. Learn how to contribute to the evolution of Consciousness.

Re-Visioning Your Profession

Ask yourself: how did I come to a professional job that has nothing much to do with how I think and how I live?

In the West, people of the eighteenth century saw the rise of the institution of democracy along with two great human institutions of capitalism and liberal education. All these institutions were idealist in their initial conceptualization; the new scientific technology fueled the engine of their growth.

Democracy is based on the spiritual idea of equality of all people. Religions and monarchy were elitist institutions and democracy was the modern liberation from elitism, or so it was conceptualized in the beginning.

Unfortunately, as explained in the previous chapters, human beings have these brain circuits of domination, and in the mid-twentieth century, some opportunists adapted the dogma of materialism for science to destroy and dominate over religions. It never quite succeeded in doing that, because spirituality is innate in us; people may get confused, but they are not going to blindly embrace a mere idea—we are material machines—to get rid of elevating ideas like love and goodness that they know have value because they do get occasional experiential glimpse of them.

However, you call it, a system with dogma grows with domination in mind, it is elitist. The religionists and aristocrats were already elitist; now they were joined by another group of elitists: the meritocrats of the higher education establishments of learning. It is they that reshaped liberal education into a job training. Initially, it was tough going, but the rise of information technology helped to make ordinary people into moronic enough to happily train for jobs, process information, and accept that as education. If it gives a degree, and a guaranteed entry to a professional job, and unlimited access to entertainment, why not?

Earlier, I (Amit) referred to the talk Professor Alan Bloom once gave on what a college graduate should know to call himself educated; then he gave a huge list of authors and their books. When somebody in the audience asked, wouldn't it take years to digest all that information? I will never forget what happened next; the professor slyly smiled and said, who said they have to be digested! Just have the info. Civilized conversation demands that. Everyone got the message! Education is gathering information so you can pretend having a lot of knowledge.

This degradation of liberal higher education into job training and meaningless information processing that neither helps you think meaning or live values that elevate life, took place rapidly with help from politicians. Values that bring sparks into life, that make life worth living disappeared from human societies. Instead, the human being became a wasteland.

How did this actually happen? Because the elitists took away your soul. In the feudal times they did it with clear subjugation and shear fear, now they were able to do it because you were already ambivalent about your values. The eighties and nineties were a battle between reductionists and holists that included systems theorists; but the holists were confused about the origin and the role of values as well because they did not have the gumption to give up on matter-based science.

Religions do not give you either the power or the ammunition to fight back the sophistication of the (pseudo-)scientific materialists, holists included.

Quantum physics gives you your power back, at least in part. It empowers you because it shows you the right way to think. It empowers you by exposing that the materialist Newtonian worldview cannot explain the new data about the living and the conscious. No worries: you are not a mechanical machine. It empowers you by opening the door to thinking Consciousness once again. It empowers you not only by proving the mechanical deterministic dogma is not universally true but also showing how your free will, your freedom to choose, works, how it is compromised by conditioning, and how to regain it.

But this is just a beginning—right thinking. The hard part—right living and right livelihood—requires hero's journey.

CHAPTER 6

Hero's Journey: Quantum Style

The archetypal journey of a spiritual hero is mythologized because it is universal going on for millennia. We all experience it sooner or later. Regardless of if we are 'woke' to spirituality or not, as we begin to get out of the base-level condition, we are part of this journey. This journey is not just an abstract concept that we might live or not.

Whenever we exit our comfort zones, we make some steps on our journey, for example when we want to be more assertive, let go of shyness etc.… it is a miniature of this archetypal journey. Every time we do it well, the journey, the big one, archetypal one becomes more accessible to us.

Joseph Campbell noticed the pattern for the hero's journey; he noticed similarities between various traditions. Campbell asserted, "The quest to find your true self is a universal quest that everyone has to walk in their own way."

Campbell wrote a very important book on the journey itself—*The hero with 1000 faces*. In this book, he put side by side essential elements of myths and noticed they are very similar, not as a narrative, but the whole story has stages easy to identify. So, he created a suggestive model.

However, it was the psychologist Carl Jung's investigation and theory that clarified all the stages of the journey the most.

Jungian Archetypes of the Collective Unconscious

Archetypes come to us via intuition and we give form to it with mental meaning and vital feeling. Carl Jung realized that both meaning and feeling can be represented by symbols and this is what humans do.

Witness what Jung said about his research: "There are forms or images of a collective nature which occur practically all over the earth as constituents of myths and at the same time, as individual products of unconscious."

Jung also realized that the part of the unconscious that has these codified symbols is not our personal unconscious but humanity's collective unconscious. Unfortunately, he introduced these symbolic representations of the archetypes without making any distinction from the original Platonic archetypes. We will call the Jungian symbols *Jungian archetypes.*

Jung maintained, "These [archetypes] are imprinted and hard-wired into our psyches." In quantum science, we look at them as universal software, embodiments of the Platonic archetypes.

Jung, following the lead of spiritual traditions has given the all the representations of the self-archetype that we make in our spiritual journey of soul-making, twelve of them: *Innocent, Every-man, Hero, Outlaw, Explorer, Creator, Ruler, Lover, Caregiver, Jester, Magician, and Sage.*

The Innocent

The innocent goes through life with what he has (the base-level human condition) without a care—a happy-go-lucky personality—driven by tamas. It takes a few incarnations, our guess, to eventually wake up to the next stage. Due to the drive towards holotropy no doubt.

Today, of course, due to mass media, power seekers manipulate the people who live in the base-level condition into expressions of their negative emotions. The term innocent hardly applies to people of economically developed countries. But you can still find them in underdeveloped countries.

The Everyman

The everyman archetype on the other hand develops the two major concerns that educated human adults have: 1) a satisfying profession that will help her belong in the society at large; and 2) a satisfying mate that will give him support throughout life. Driven by these concerns and the suffering that the lack of fulfillment of these concerns bring, these people begin to search for meaning and purpose and eventually intuit the existence of the archetypes and realize that there is an archetypal world out there to explore which will enable him or her to improve lot beyond the base-level human condition and bring meaning, purpose, fulfillment, and satisfaction.

The everyman stage starts within THE ORDINARY WORLD—the hero/heroine begins amidst everyday life—he/she is still unaware of what is ahead. It is a context that is familiar to everyone, that speaks about our personality—we are the hero of our unique journey. We start somewhere. We see our strengths and limitations. But we are not oblivious any more of the feeling that something is not alright; we just feel that something must happen to make it alright. There is some cry in our heart for something new, for adventure, for the unexpected, something that goes beyond our ordinary life. It's a call for adventure in the direction of our dreams.

For example, try to remember how you felt before meeting a person you fell in love with; that's the kind of feeling we are talking about, that you should look for. Soon you leap to the third stage; you have become a hero.

Hero's Journey Proper Begins with the Awakening of the Hero Stage

After exploration of the everyman stage, comes the stage of which the Jungian archetype is properly called the Hero and the rest of the Jungian representations of the self-identity codify the stages of the hero's journey as a person goes through it (fig. 5).

*Figure 5. The Hero: Prince Gautama who later became Buddha
Albert Einstein who began his life as a scientist as an outsider later
became the hero of 20th century science.*

It starts with the CALL FOR ADVENTURE—not anyone at any time can follow this journey proper. For this step we are not yet ready, so we need to wait. Until when? Until that call for adventure comes and is very loud. This need for change becomes clear. For example—through a shift in perspective, we see differently, or maybe it's a call for action that cannot be postponed. Life as usual or business as usual cannot continue. Usually this can be a life change, a threat, a loss, an accident, a loss in carrier, something that jeopardizes the life of the hero or of the community. It can also be just a revelation of the source of an old issue that was bothering us. Something that will shake up our world. So, on one hand, we might feel threatened, cornered, boxed, but on the other hand we feel much more alive.

For me (Amit), it was the crystallization experience when the question came to me, *Why do I live this way?* and the answer followed, *I don't have to.* I have to integrate how I think, live, and make my living. The experience was telling me my dharma for this life—the archetype of wholeness.

It's a wake-up call, always. Now we are summoned to an adventure. This call can be intense, fast, acute, and can come in various ways. Sometimes this call to adventure is not comfortable.

Our transformation starts as a seed that grows in the darkness of our unconscious. And this seed tells us that we have to do something, but it's not clear. It's the possibility of a new us, me, you. And this awakens us to a new possibility of being, feeling, doing and this inspires us to take action to something enlightening. It is where our transformation can begin. Transformation is up to us, our decision also determines how far we can go.

There is a difference between change and transformation, as I (Valentina) have learnt from meditation teacher, Adinathananda, while he was presenting his take on the hero's journey, following Joseph Campbell's work.

All transformation is change but not all change is transformation. If change happens to your house, you can still recognize what was before, even the step-by-step detail of the change—maybe something is now smaller, maybe there is a change in color, maybe you changed the furniture in one room. But transformation is a full-scale remodeling of the house. The word "transform" means to go beyond—trans + form, beyond form. Its form and also structure alters fundamentally in a discontinuous way so that it is impossible to pinpoint the change in a step-by-step way.

Taoism gives the model of caterpillar and butterfly. Change is when the caterpillar worm just grows. But transformation—the butterfly is totally different.

The human equivalent of this shift is to our identity—what we identify with that reflects our character. Our identity is all the this and that which follows after we say "I am". For example, you can refer to a biological aspect—short, thin; or a role assumed—child, mother, teacher, or say, I am optimistic. Which ones reflect your embodied values, your character?

Remember this: transformation is dynamic and fluid and is wide in range. We make choices every single day, consciously or not. Every new choice we make is an invitation to a new experience which can take us out of the comfort zone and help us transform. Often in unimaginable ways. Transformative life begins when we get out of our comfort zones. Just by challenging our identities (role etc.), we can go inwards and at the same time outward, in order to express our potentialities in life. To really live is to transform. We are always experiencing a phase of this path to wholeness.

Campbell classified transformation in 3 types. In general, he said people transform as a result of 3 major causes: 1. Trauma; 2. Unexpected powerful experiences; 3. Consciously intended transformation.

1. A trauma can appear unexpected, a crisis, an accident, death of a dear one, or a diagnosis of a potentially lethal disease, etc. We can't stay the same as we were, we can't continue as usual. This is the cause for those who were not willing to transform until the traumatic event.

2. The 2nd—is based on surprise, not traumatic but unexpected. Campbell describes 2 types here. First type—totally unanticipated—you were doing your work as usual and a brother you haven't seen for 40 years show up at your door. This is an unexpected but pleasant effect. Or let's say you get an unforeseen promotion. This kind of events can be powerful, they occur unexpectedly and when you are engaged in an ordinary activity and not expecting anything life altering.

The second kind of surprises are the ones that happen when we are in an activity that is out of the norm—example: we visit an ancient temple in India that is very special; or we visit our childhood place after thirty years. At the outset of this one-time experience, you anticipate it might be intense, you prepare for its possible power, you can even speculate for it—that trip to India will transform you, but you are not looking for transformation, what you overtly want is just an adventure. This kind of trigger of transformation also occurs as a surprise. Amit's experience referred to above belongs to this kind. He was at a professional conference.

3. This is the best of the three. Using intentions. Choosing transformation on purpose. We consciously seek for an experience that will lead us to transform. Any spiritual practice is such a choice. Meditations leading to a very first Samadhi, vital energy practices precipitating the movement of kundalini to a higher chakra, belong to this category. Here our primary motivation is to transform, and this is the difference from the ones before. You have been listening for the waking call of this step of the journey. This call is like a scream in your heart. It's not possible to stay the same anymore. Or maybe you just realized that your life as currently configured is not fulfilling. You are a bit confused on what you want but you set out to find it anyway.

When we pursue transformation consciously, we listen closely to our aspirations. We can be distracted by of ego to some possible escapes for scenarios that will offer us adventure. Or we can practice yoga try to find some great sage for guidance.

Transformation doesn't happen in an instant. The journey of the hero is not a one-weekend event, it's an ongoing process. Transformation takes time, and many times it occurs so slowly that looking through your day-to-day life, you don't even see it. Unless you know the clues to look for. When you do certain forms of meditation, for example, you know where to look to notice.

Transformation involves two cycles, the first is the transformational process itself; the 2nd is called the integrative cycle or more aptly hero's return: how you digest, assimilate your experience, how you integrate your new and healthier self, getting rid of old distracting patterns, which is not easy. These aspects hold negative emotions that we have avoided or rejected for long, like anger, fear, shame, anxiety. The innermost part of this process entails a genuine emotional alchemy that starts with an emotional surrender, a birth of a new self, an identity with a new character.

Transformation means always a radical change, not just adding or modifying a bit of this and that habit; that is change. Transformation is radical change of character. We might not be ready for this dramatic alteration of our personality.

Also note this: Being unprepared doesn't mean we are not good enough. It is just that the process of readiness is unconscious. A seed will stay dormant in the soil until good conditions arise. When a flower starts to grow, it will not grow faster if you pull it. It needs its own time. We need the right conditions in order for transformation to occur, and we choose every day what kind of choice—to grow or have a passive fatalistic attitude

In order to be proactive, we need to identify in which areas of our life we don't feel we are fulfilling our needs, because our dissatisfaction is not accidental, it's a sign that something from there will bring something, a test, to push us toward transformation.

We need preparation as well for the big challenges ahead of us on our spiritual journey. So, when a call comes, it means you are ready, you can start your journey, you have what you need for a safe and complete journey, the journey of your life—from one mode of existence to another radically different mode.

The Beginning of the Journey

The first three stages of the hero's journey proper—Rebel, Explorer, and Creator—set the context of the journey: the rebel realizes that one who has to break out from the existing conditioned ways of the society no matter that he will become an outsider; the explorers begin to explore new meaning and soon discover that new meaning comes with purpose which is dictated by an archetype which they now make the focus of their investigation. The creators then go about the creative journey of finding new meaning of value.

The Rebel

The rebel stage (fig. 6) needs to be properly understood. For children, being a rebel is part of gaining autonomy. But for an adult, it does not happen immediately. One hears the call, one aspires. Then in a bizarre way appears A REFUSAL OF THE CALL, a postponement really.

We are facing some fears that begin to arise, regardless of if we are walking already or resisting it. So, first is the call—yes, let's do it, and then—"wait a bit". It's a normal reaction. Nothing bad in itself. But if you wait too long, you may even have to start from stage one. Many people do this. For example—you want to jump in water from 1-2 meters high, if you don't jump at first and you wait, you will not jump, fear will arise, maybe you think—friends may be laughing at you if you failetc. So it's a fear arising from self-questioning or self-doubt—you have second thoughts—after an enthusiastic yes.

Figure 6. Robin Hood, the quintessential rebel

Feelings may arise for not wanting to leave the comfort of life; why go there, for what? To start this now, or go for a new job where I have no friends etc. This familiarity keeps you here. Initially, the adventure seems exciting and now something triggers the question—is this truly the adventure I seek for? We have the tendency to refuse the call and find reasons for not doing it. When you think of having the adventure of your life, even biologically your brain will emit dopamine and other hormones, but also fear will activate, searching for dangers. This is just meant to keep us alive. Fear is not designed to stop us from following our dreams, even if it may look like that. It needs to only increase our sensors to search for threats etc.—but most people stay too long in this fear state, and we start thinking of all the worst scenarios, then we come up with reasons to refuse this adventure. Rational fear is legitimate. But you need to pay attention to irrational fear based on our limiting beliefs. So, whenever feararises, remember that this is to keep you safe—ok, do it, absolutely, just be careful, do it properly, be safe, not in an extremely optimistic way without engaging the rational brain.

The mythological story of Percival and the holy grail illustrates how fear of breaking the convention make sus hesitate. Percival saw that the grail king is sick; in fact, the whole kingdom is afflicted by some kind of sickness, but being an aspiring knight, he bent to the custom of not opening your mouth. It took him six years of exploration to become a rebel and ask, "What's wrong here?

Practice: Self-Observation

There are practices to help us cross this threshold of fear and be sure it is alright to do that. If we let fear choose for us, it's a bad choice. Fear should work for us, not the other way around. So, first we make sure of the nature of the call. If it's good, how to be sure you go in a correct way on the path?

Do you feel inspiration growing in your heart and this being aligned with the movement of consciousness? Then, *step one—noticing*.

There is usually a feeling of refusal in our heart to that call or a desire to fall away and not engage. Seek out for what is on the other side, don't take sides, just notice what is happening in your consciousness, pros and cons regarding this initiative. The stage doesn't need to take too long. It's happening right now—you do it when you're facing this inner conflict.

So, you collect data from both sides. Like it's a parliament and you have 2 opposite parties. *Then: step 2*: connect to yourself, the real you. Ground your awareness into the present moment. How? By following your breath—the classical method to keep your awareness in the here and now. Take a deep breath and allow yourself to experience the moment. When you feel present here and now, connect to the reason you're afraid to follow that call—you're ready now to see clearly what that fear or reluctance tells you, the real message.

You're grounded. Is the outcome that you desire more than this experiencing a momentary discomfort? You're weighing each side. Now you can do that. You have collected the information and now you're neutral, you're in a balanced state and step three: you ask—is my anticipation of the fruit—what I can find etc. if I follow this call greater than this discomfort that I feel now? If yes, you go to the next stage. If no, maybe you are not ready, maybe it's about commitment to some principles or ideas that you are not ready to follow right away. Then, you observe your field of awareness as a witness, everything in that field at once, with compassion, and without exercising any option. Even this attitude can trigger a shift in your decision. So, the practice is to just notice what you feel but without responding. Self-observation—with the objective to recognize your patterns and all the narratives they create.

You wrap our experiences in all kinds of narratives—I am angry because this guy said… but truly although that is what triggered your anger, it actually has a deeper cause. The narratives are created by the self-defense mechanisms of the ego. The best thing about self-observation is that in the moment when you really notice these patterns, you're free of them. Caution: You might get a break from one pattern but there are many. The same pattern can have many nuances, you just saw one, but are still unaware of others, so you may have to repeat the process. When the level of freedom is much greater and you have the feeling—now I am clear—then move on.

There will appear a shift in perspective—the moment of yes or no. In order to make sure you exhaust all reasons why you shouldn't do that—ask yourself—am I transgressing any spiritual principles that I'm aware of by doing this? If yes, stop. The antidote is to create a new perspective, reframe your experience—while you are chal-lenged, see where this can lead you. What is my perspective on this situation? For example—is this for me an opportunity to grow, or is it to get rid of my loneliness? This shift in perspective is a tool to use whenever our ego tries to affect our decision making. This is when we break free of the fears that keep us in a state of confusion, indecision, uncertainty. Now it's clear, I know what to do.

Preparation for the next Step: The fundamental quantum principles you need to learn to live in the quantum way

Nonlocality: understanding the nature of consciousness

Analysis shows that two waves of possibility, when they interact locally, coming close, they go into a special state of correlation of entanglement, they become able to communicate with each other instantly. Instant communication is nonlocal.

Example: Does nonlocality seem like an esoteric concept? It should not be. Many times, you are thinking of a friend, and the friend calls you on your cell, how do such events happen? Nonlocality, in this case mental telepathy.

Another example: Five-year old Einstein is sick in this hospital. His father brings him a compass. Young Albert is fascinated, how does the needle always point to the north? Suddenly, he is taken over by the thought: the universe is reaching out to me. That fascination about the universe never left him and guided all his research. We call such events synchronicity, an example of nonlocality. They, too, are examples of nonlocality revealing mysterious correlations that guide our lives.

Realize that nonlocality—signal less communication—is really a oneness of the communicating objects. The domain of potentiality outside of space and time is a domain of Oneness. This is Consciousness in its attribute of *sat*—existence, truth.

Furthermore, analysis shows that quantum measurement leads to both a subject and an object, the measurer and the measured from the quantum possibilities of Consciousness. This is the attribute of chit—awareness. Awareness is manifest Consciousness.

Surprised? Small children, when they close their eyes and the world disappears, think that they have disappeared too; you cannot see them. Amazing, no? Quantum physics is agreeing with children's intuition.

Child development theorists traditionally make the child wrong and teach them that NO, the child does not disappear when he closes eyes; instead, they should say, YES, it is true without an object to experience the subject/self, the experiencer also disappears. But don't get the idea your body disappears into nihilism; it just goes into potentiality. We can see your body, we can collapse its potentiality even when are not doing it.

As adult, you assume a lot of things that upon examination, prove to be blinders making it difficult to comprehend reality—what is really the case. This is especially true about the reality that quantum physics is revealing for us. You need to have a child's mind, beginner's mind to appreciate quantum physics.

The third defining quality of consciousness is that subject/self that you experience in everyday life, a constriction of consciousness is not a permanent state; when we experience love or beauty it readily expands, and we experience that as joy or happiness—*ananda*.

We have gone over these ideas before. We are repeating because now is your time to internalize them.

Collapse, Choice, and Purpose, Downward causation

Collapse is the preferred name physicists give to this phenomenon of actualization or manifestation of possibilities.

Choice is a causal agent of change. How does Consciousness inject purpose in the affairs of the world? Through its choice that precipitates collapse. All living beings must evolve towards purposive movements that are part and parcel of the laws of Consciousness.

Remind yourself especially: Quantum collapse is due to Consciousness, a nonmaterial agency. Material interactions can only convert possibility into other possibilities, never actuality. This is called von Neumann's theorem. Noting that material interactions are example of upward causation—cause rises upward from elementary particle to atoms to molecules to bulk matter—sometimes we refer to conscious choice as downward causation which is how religions conceive God to create the world.

Interaction between objects can only produce possibilities; it is higher nonlocal Consciousness that is the ultimate creator (called God in religion) via downward causation.

Discontinuity

Remember and internalize another principle in play—discontinuity: Material interaction among material possibilities produce change in a continuous way; they can be calculated using the mathematics of calculus. Collapse—change of possibility into actuality—is discontinuous, cannot be calculated by any means.

How do you understand discontinuity? How do you practice for it? Try to live with the uncertainty of not knowing what it means exactly, while mulling over the idea in your mind again and again. Just like that, you will fall into the quantum self and understanding will happen. Like an awakening.

Tangled Hierarchy

Learn something new as well: there is one more quantum principle in play in the game of creation. Think of the process of manifestation: Consciousness chooses, potentiality is collapsed to actuality. But the choosing Consciousness is the unmanifest ground of being, no separateness there. When the object actualizes, Consciousness does too, it identifies with the observer's brain and becomes a self, separate from the object of its experience.

The mystery behind the brain's capacity to be a kind of playground for manifest Consciousness, that is you and I, is the mechanism of tangled hierarchy, a circular relationship between the brain apparatuses involved.

Deeper analysis beyond the scope of this book shows that the crucial brain apparatuses are those of perception and memory. You can see the play of tangled hierarchy between them, can't you? There is memory without perception, perception is needed to create memory. But think! Memory is needed for perception; memory creates perception of what previously was unmanifest.

So, this is the fourth important quantum principle: tangled hierarchy, circular relationship.

Example: Ordinary relationships you are used to are simple hierarchical, either you dominate or the other dominates. But once in a while, you get into a relationship where at least momentarily, it seems like neither of you are dominating, you and he have become part of a whole where when you begin and he ends has become blurred. This is tangled hierarchy. Practice this with your existing relationships that you respect. Again, wait for understanding to dawn.

Have you read Hermann Hesse's beautiful novel *Siddhartha*? In the seventies America, somebody made a movie of it. In a scene, the protagonist hero, Siddhartha, is in love with a paramour and wants a date. The paramour asks: why should I date you? Siddhartha says: I can think; I can fast, and I can wait. That convinces the lady.

Say you have materialist friend who challenges: how do you know that you are not a machine, you can change, move beyond your conditioned programs? Even more importantly, how do you earn the trust of your students.

Now you know what to say to your friend:

1. I can choose new vital and mental software from archetypal intuitions and creative insights.

2. I can correlate with you and communicate with you non-locally with telepathy.

3. I can love you; it expands my experience of conscious awareness and I experience joy.

4. I can take a quantum leap of creative insight (and teach you the trick too).

5. I can make tangled hierarchical relationship with others, especially you.

Gaining Confidence in Your New Perspective: Living with Quantum Uncertainty

This new perspective will have to be solidified. You need to establish clear boundaries with your patterns. Only now this is possible, now that you have discovered you're in charge, and not the self-sabotaging conditioned system of your Newtonian brain.

You discover you're empowered by the previous stages. You will feel this very clearly. You feel that you can draw a line the conditioned patterns can't cross. Doesn't sound so logical, but it is like that. It happens.

And then—you integrate. You allow the new perspective to become part of you. With the new perspective you start to understand what it means to get comfortable being uncomfortable, to be comfortable with uncertainty. People are afraid of uncertainty, but somehow you need to go there, even if it's an unknown territory, outside of your comfort zone, you don't have anything familiar there. You should get used to that, get comfortable with that, because it defines the moment after awakening.

Only if you are awake can you cope with uncertainty. What you discover here is that you're much more equipped now to face the challenge, you have the resilience needed. You let the new you be. Manifestation. You're not the same person you were before. We now have another dominant resonance, we see the world differently, as enchanted. This is an ongoing process, not a one-timeevent. You discover that when life gives you uncomfortable opportunities to grow, you can meet these challenges gracefully, and this is what will happen from now on.

We can face tough moments when we are cornered by our fears; we may need to regroup and get the power to go in a safe and proper way. This is the real reason for our natural reaction, this 2nd thought reaction. It's nothing evil, just do not stay in it too long. Let this mechanism protect you and then respond. When the going gets tough, the tough gets going, but it is ok to wait until you feel the power inside you before you get going.

The Explorer: Discovering the Science of Manifestation— part 1—the Three I's

The First I: Inspiration

You are now ready to face the actual challenges. So far, they were just assumptions and theories about the challenges. Now you enter the real path—experience and exploration (fig. 7). You cannot do it alone. In all cultures, no one makes this journey alone. You need a guide, a mentor, before you go beyond the known. completely unknown territory. So, this stage begins with MEETING YOUR GUIDE, a person who has done it. This person's presence in your life gives you a crucial element of the quantum science of manifestation—inspiration.

*Figure 7. Nobody represents the motto of the explorer –
to go where no body has gone before – better than
Captain Kirk of Star Trek fame.*

You have solidified yourself with your new quantum worldview and now you're above your fears of uncertainty. You didn't say no to the call of the archetypes, and you clearly proved yourself worthy to go further. After the stage of the rebel, a mentor shows up, in person or through the Internet, in order to offer advice, insight, training to the hero/heroine to make sure they keep away from those initial fears, and this synchronicity can be a very empowering moment of inspiration. What might have seemed impossible alone now it does not; imagine yourself without a compass or food in a jungle and then suddenly food appears, direction appears where to go. In this way, this is a very empowering moment because the impossible now seems perfectly possible with the wisdom of one who has walked the path before.

The mentor sees possibilities in the hero that the hero does not see. For some, the mentor may not even be a stable presence in one's life. Or mentors can be several providing multiple different moments of inspiration.

A mentor can also be a friend, or a complete stranger we meet in a plane who gives us advice. Maybe they don't even know why they tell you things, but for you it's an aha moment.

This mentor, guide, can have many forms. It's a multifaceted manifestation of reality. The forms may not always be human. It can be an advertising panel that can trigger in you a wow, this is what I have to do. You can't miss that moment, when it happens it's powerful. The transfer of power—not from the panel, that's just a trigger.

I (Amit) was once driving alone long distance—tired and out of focus—Is it all worth it? I turned on the radio to keep me awake, and guess what? A Christian evangelist was giving a sermon. In booming voice, he said, "Why do you insist being the chairman of your life? Give the gavel to the holy spirit." This was exactly what I needed to hear; this is also how inspirations can come, from unexpected sources.

You now connect in a fundamental way to the archetypal journey. And if you look back to what happened so far in your life, for sure you can easily identify such mentors and/or such moments of inspiration. You are talking with someone or listening to someone, and some inspiration can rise at the right time, when you're ready.

The mentor can open the path, using various tools called initiations, something the hero has not yet recognized. When we are empowered with the tools we need, then only, our journey can begin in full force. This is the power of initiation.

In tantra initiation means to give power to someone, empowering her. When you are initiated, you have power. Initiation is not just explaining principles, explaining the ritual; it isa power transfer; an awakening. They offer insight and wisdom for the whole journey ahead and help the hero see life in a new way.

In quantum science, we have discovered the science of manifestation; it is part and parcel of quantum science. Based on it, we have developed a scientific ritual. But before the ritual can be taught, we have to go through a mini stage that can be called TURNING OBSTACLES INTO OPPORTUNITIES.

Turning Obstacles into Opportunities, Finding Meaning in Adversity

What is the principle of practice here? We face mostly internal adversity. Our fears, and problems. What happens in the outer world mirrors our inner world. We are stepping in a world where we are cocreating. What is this, makes no sense, why is this happening to me? Finding meaning in adversity is a golden key to pass successfully this difficult stage of archetypal journey.

Struggles may force us to engage. Finding meaning in adversity will lead us from the ego-based belief that *life is happening to us* to a new superior one: **life is happening for us.** Courage to face obstacles and shadows, small ones and then bigger ones.

Problems may force us to engage life with more important questions. Suffering can make us compassionated and give us a chance to care.

Welcoming what's happening in our life, despite ego s like or dislike, welcoming everything alleviates suffering. We always receive the lesson we can handle, nothing more, this is a universal law in all traditions. In Christianity there is a saying: God never gives you as a burden more than you can carry. We are meant to grow.

When we hide out in a non-learning, non-growing life, we do not get lessons because we are stuck into a non-growing style. These lessons that may involve a letting go, they never are punishments. They are simply meant to take us further.

Agreed, this is a hard way to move further. And they will require all attention, they can't be ignored. This hard way happens to us because unconsciously we refuse to accept an easy-to-follow invite to grow, transform. You may kick and scream when you're first awoken, like a person that is woken up by someone from a deep sleep, you may not understand why you are woken up. You need to let the experience unfold, and you will begin to understand that this is an opportunity, and even more, you will also have gratitude for it. What appeared at first as a punishment (why is this happening to me? what have I done? why me?) now it's a major breakthrough, and you feel gratitude, you're awake and can realize finally that you were helped, it was a wake-up call, it was not what you were thinking. Transformation comes when we learn these lessons.

When something like this happens, of course, in the beginning we are angry, upset, but what we need to do is only to pay attention because with the right attitude, in this moment, very tough corner at this stage, these difficult events are coming for a reason. So, this hard way is because we didn't follow the easy way.

Native American tradition says: "the soul would have no rainbow if the eyes had no tears" (message: find meaning in adversity). All the beauty you see due to rain is the beauty we obtain when we learn the lesson.

If we are simply aware and can examine what happens in our life with openness and simply let that event talk to us instead of projecting on what's happening various ideas and blames, we might discover beauty or other qualities and universal energy in the event, assets for our personal transformation.

The idea is not that we mandatorily have to pass through traumatic events. But only if we refuse to understand in gentler ways.

If we are stubbornly refusing to progress, say no no no…even when others tell you that you don't have a good attitude in this and you still don't care. Instead, you say to the universe "I am stubborn, I don't want to do anything, I can't change." And the universe will take the message that you want the hard way. Unfortunately, most people get it the hard way—*via negativa.*

Finding meaning in any adversity has important human and spiritual values. It can lift us to a higher level, makes us better people. Even to expressing gratitude after the fact. Many people get transformation after suffering and set back. If you ask them—do you have any regrets? They will say, "What happened made me the man/woman I am now, so I feel gratitude. If it wasn't for that, I wouldn't be who I am now, and I would have repeated same mistakes etc."

Here we can't keep any mask, all masks fall away, the real self emerges. Such events also help us accept our own limitations, we become more vulnerable and come down from the pedestal we have set ourselves on. We recognize that on our own we are not enough. No matter how strong our ego is, there will always be another one more powerful.

Sharing our limitations with another can be the first step to simplicity and to overcoming the distress we pass through. Being aware of the limitations will reinforce or awaken the nonlocal connection with others, in quantum science we identify this nonlocal connection as our empathy, an ability to experience others' problems without identifying with them. When people feel loved their life changes. These events will transform our heart as well. Empathy will increase.

Finding meaning in adversity is not like finding a solution to a puzzle, nor a simple phrase resuming all. It has to be a profound experience. Otherwise, one may tell you anything, but it's just theory, you don't get to the real meaning, it's just empty words. You need to have a deep experience, then you say, yes, now I know, now I understand.

Finding meaning in adversity can be also an important path to happiness. We all want that. The test we pass through will lead us to maturity, will help us care for others and give us better knowledge.

There is this study done by Alfred Adler, famous psychologist. He discovered that often some perceived disadvantages, such as problems we know we have, prove to be disguised advantages because they force us discover abilities that would have stayed dormant forever. Only as we compensate for these disadvantages that our greatest gifts are revealed. Adler did quite a big study with a large number of people; he discovered that 70% of the students who were studying visual art (painting, sculpture) had eye anomalies. He discovered that great composers, Mozart, Beethoven, had degenerative disease in their hearing mechanism. And he also cited many other examples, from a wide variety of vocations of those who discovered new strengths because of their congenital disadvantages. And he concluded that perceived disadvantages such as birth defects, physical ailments, poverty, etc. can be really like springboards to success. And that success is not achieved in spite of those disadvantages but because of those. This gives another light on finding meaning in adversity.

Our greatest advantages may not be what we think. They could be hidden in disadvantages. One key is to identify those disadvantages through a careful and sometimes painful self-observation. Why painful? Because of the ego. The ego hates to be unmasked, to be exposed in all its weakness and ugliness. Ego puts personality masks, self-images, this is me, but it's like a billboard telling you a slogan. The self-inventory requires total honesty and not all are able to do so. How to admit that I am like that? I am not, the others are.

So finally, remember this: your strengths are hidden within your weaknesses. Your advantages are hidden within disadvantages.

Enemies and Allies

Challenges appear; they are called TEST/CHALLENGES or ALLIES/ENEMIES by Joseph Campbell. The hero has fully emerged out of his former life. No turning back. They wouldn't accept to be the same guy they were before. Regardless of what happens. But the old ways of living are not dead; there are people in the hero's life living in their old ways that overlap with the hero's life and they oppose the hero's change of course, his ideas of transformation. The enemies can be such people as well, but they actually are mostly internal—fears unconsciously programmed along the way; they can be self-imposed limitations, sabotaging habits that pull us back. Like in jail, centuries ago, they had big heavy chains on prisoners so they could not run. So, these are the enemies trying to bring you back to where you were.

What does the hero need now? To stay steadfast in the plan to unlearn what she practiced all her life?

In conditioned life, we learnt how to defend ourselves, all the lies and narratives we told ourselves to justify our decisions; we did this all our life, we were experts, so now we need to unlearn all that. The ego becomes a challenging source of obstacles thrown at the hero. Amidst this, the hero discovers he needs help; he has friends and allies to help. They also discover they have enemies.

Do these friends and enemies have any purpose? Both categories will teach the hero various lessons and these lessons are part of what is to come in the future. Heroes learn new skills and obtain a deeper vision, wisdom on how they can transform themselves.

Realize this: Tests are never a punishment; they come to strengthen and prepare you for the adventure ahead. Especially now when you need to be really focused on the archetypal journey, way more than before, because the next big step is to be a creator.

Allies can be some inner energies you didn't know you had and now they awaken. They can be other people as well, sharing some of the same ideas, aspirations, and a similar path. They may have different strengths and you can support one another. Maybe they don't have what you have either; then it's a win-win situation. You both are motivated by the same idea—transformation. No competition. Nor is it just a gathering of people sharing the same interest. Heroes develop with these allies a state of harmony to feel connected.

Kaula

A very important practice that I (Valentina) learnt from Adinathananda, meditation teacher, is to create "your sacred/spiritual community" *kaula* or *kula* in Sanskrit. In order to make community with your allies, a special link is required. Not like making friends in general, this is qualitatively different. A *kaula* is basically a community of the heart. It is a resource on the path to become more authentic. People in a sacred community *kaula* can talk to you and you with them with radical honesty. They are willing to stick with you in hard times. And also celebrate with you in great times. And you too with them. They are the people who simply help you clean up the mess you may produce now and them. They can help you connect to your authentic self: they call it when they see you being inauthentic; they celebrate when they see you as you really are. They are always willing to shed a light on your blind spots and you on theirs.

The moments you are affected by these blind spots, they are there to help, willing to listen to you in a way much deeper than a surface conversation, and they are with you in order to enjoy the simplest moment of life, laugh with you. Being with the people of your community, you don't feel the need to pretend a behavior or persona; or to be different than you really are. It's like being alone and being in such a group is the same, nothing artificial. All is based on values and authenticity.

So, it is very different from how we relate to just friends. With friends you have fun, you feel good. What you have is a pleasure bond. But a sacred community is a much deeper bond; it is a connection of nonlocality. People are friends for a reason—a common goal, then they separate; or for a season—maybe they grew up together, go the same high school or college, a season together, developing a bond that doesn't persist in time. But a sacred community is for a lifetime; in fact, often for more than one lifetime.

You can call such a bond unconditional friendship—not for a reason or not for a few seasons, but forever. In such a community we become more authentic and are not afraid or ashamed or scared to be ourselves and speak up our mind. We can see that the choices we make affect others and the other way around. We can honor each other's gifts instead of focusing on faults. We can see our own patterns, can highlight the potential in others and help them grow. Such *kaula* will support us in moments of success but also when we are out of alignment.

Practice

This is a small exercise—a dynamic one—for objectifying your own potential *kaula* community. Who is to be included in your heart community of *kaula*?

You need to draw a circle. Place a dot in the circle. The dot is you. Inside the circles, mark with dots people that you think might be in such a community, people you feel you can connect at the necessary deep level. People you potentially feel you can have the necessary heart to heart connection. You can also use various colors but it's not essential. Place dots for the people who belong to your community according to how close you feel to them; the points are closer to the center or more towards the circumference. Take your time to do this while we explain why this exercise can be helpful. The circle and the placement of dots can change in time, maybe more dots will come, maybe some will disappear—it's just how you feel about this now, at this very moment.

Outside the circle place other dots for some people who are in your regular usual community, friends, family, but you don't feel they are part of your spiritually transformative nonlocally-connected community. You now can see the difference, how it is to have such a close connection with someone as in a *kaula*. Even with a family member, you may not feel the same, maybe not even with a lover who is on the same path as you. After you labeled the numbers, here is the exercise to objectify our potentiality to create or discover such a group. You need to answer fast, without thinking much:

1. Did you expect that your friends and your *kaula* group would overlap?

2. What are some qualities you appreciate in your *kaula* community (very brief)—actual or potential—what you would like to have. These would be about your allies. Also, it will show in what direction you need most the allies.

3. What are some qualities you appreciate about your friends, generally? Here also you will see what you need (like loyalty, stability, whatever you're grateful for). A process of becoming aware what kind of allies we need and also what we need to develop in ourselves.

4. How do those in your sacred community help you— maybe they stand up for you, help you in tough moments, you know the best what to write here. This answer emphasizes the actions and roles of your allies, and you can identify various projections or replicas of your fundamental archetypal journey in your daily life.

5. How do those in your *kaula* help you transform? Reflect on a few events when someone helped you a lot, not just to feel good, but to transform. Maybe it was not pleasant at first, but you transformed regardless. This way you

become aware of the truth in your assumptions that these people are in your *kaula*. This is a crucial question. If you can't find even one example of such help, this person does not belong in your *kaula*, she is just friends.

6. How do *you* support those in your *kaula* group? Because it is a two-way connection. For example—what is one small thing you can do today or tomorrow to show your appreciation to them. Fast answer, not filtered by mind or ego?

7. What keeps you caring for one another? See what you think—is it love, common aspiration, respect, or something else?

8. (a surprising but meaningful question) Who or What else would you include in your *kaula* group—you can put everything you think that might help—they can be heroes from movies, guides from ancient times, animals, plants, anything you would like to have nearby in your *kaula* heart group. The answer is relevant because it shows some deep aspirations you have, as well as ideals, qualities, virtues you would like to have. Sooner or later some allies having these qualities may show up.

9. Is God always present in your *kaula* group, and if yes, what impact does this have on you?

Another practice: Personal Archeology

Looking back on your life, connect the dots in the exercise above. The dots are not only people, but they are also defining moments in your life. Some are big, and they have been forever there. Some are little ones. All of them reveal our soul prints. When connecting the dots, recollect various life situations and put together different places, people, situations; going far enough in the past you can identify which are your earliest memories, and then who were the major influencers in your life. Or what major events, both good and bad have marked those past years. As you reflect on those memories, what lessons did you learn because of them, consciously or not? What did they reveal about you? Notice how apparently insignificant events for one can change the entire trajectory for another. Like passing comets– at some point they can have prophetic effects. They can change your global view on life.

So far we discussed the allies. What about enemies? This is equally important. Here we deal mostly with anger. Tibetan and Indian tantra say anger is the greatest enemy of meditation. It's impossible to reach stillness when anger is running around. *Vajrayana* tradition says the hardest thing to do is to stop yourself from getting angry when an enemy, especially an intimate one, presses the right buttons.

To stop anger just when it's exploding is like standing in front of a moving train, it will run you over. What to do in order to control this energy that is one of the worst? There are several approaches. Some of them aim for a gradual and slow process, some of them—radical.

Tibetan Practice– This method is to meditate/reflect on how anger gives you only harm—you can't sleep at night, it makes you unpleasant to be around, you're not welcome in that state. No friends. The whole world looks dark. So, you need to meditate about this in advance.

Another method: when anger is happening—do some alchemical method or sublimate the energy from lower chakras to higher ones using pranayama or chi gong.

In tantra, the idea is to channelize the energy of that negative emotion, here, anger, to something positive. But you need to prepare the ascending path, called the *sushumna nadi* in Sanskrit; this requires vital creativity. Alternatively you can practice giving, forgiving, etc. Once you have made some positive emotional brain circuits, practice watching your negative emotions as they arise, THIS TOO SHALL PASS.

Give up the victim mindset. Blaming others is a stupid attitude. The spiritual teacher Shantideva said—it's like blaming the stick for hitting you. If one comes hitting you with a stick, you shouldn't blame the stick. We do this every single time when we blame others for what happens to us. Victims are always losers in life; you're disempowering yourself as such. "I would do that but I can't because of her or him or the government…". You give the power of your life's decisions to someone else; and you keep being a poor victim, just blaming others.

Instead, you can be mature and gradually shift your perspective from "this is happening to me", to "this is happening for me". Just change of one word but it makes a huge difference in attitude, in the state of consciousness. We need to keep this in mind so we can alchemize.

The Crucial New Tool: Intention

The big question of empowerment, the one that really turns people on to quantum physics, is, do we really create reality? If our deep Consciousness—Oneness—is the ground of all being—manifest and unmanifest—then it must also be that Oneness creates the manifest world of our experience. So far it is still about what ancient people called God the creator. But quantum physics gave us the observer effect. Then is a corollary question arises where it becomes personal: "Do I create my own reality? Can I? Give me the secret."

The physicist Fred Alan Wolf created the intriguing phrase in the seventies that turned many people on to quantum physics, "We create our own reality," said he. People were energized, entire sectors of religion were chanting reality-making mantras, "Oh God, give me a Cadillac." Many people were claiming that their power of intention made a vegetable garden in desert soil. Gradually though, by and large people ended up disappointed.

But the question still continued to intrigue people. Then a book appeared, *The Secret* and became a best seller. Make a wish and wait patiently. Said the author. Simple enough. The message of the book got a boost from a documentary of the same name, also watched by many people.

So now that we have a fully developed quantum science of Consciousness, what does science really say? Is there a science of manifestation? What are the new rules that we need to play by?

Quantum Science of Manifestation

We begin with a Question: *How do we create our reality? Through those quantum principles?*

Answer: Yes, we create our own reality but not in our ordinary state of the ego but in the state of Oneness. The oneness is not inaccessible though to you in your ego; fortunately, you are not bound by the ordinary ego state of your Consciousness. Use the quantum principles to learn how to get the access to the creating Consciousness.

The secret of manifestation of your intentions is 1) make sure your intention is compatible with the purposive movement of Consciousness; 2) make sure to feel that your intention is compatible with the purposive movement of Consciousness and 3) make sure you have at least some access to the choosing Consciousness.

This is part of the science behind the secret of manifestation—real empowerment. One more big question remains though. What kind of stuff do we intend for, that has a better chance for manifestation? This is the subject of a subsequent next section.

Knowing What to Choose, What Not to Choose

Now some more aspects of the science of manifestations should become clear. What can we manifest by choosing? Not macro material stuff; as much as I want a new car, I cannot get a car to manifest in my garage and not in the owner's car lot by wishing it. Not that a car is not quantum possibility when nobody is looking, but it just takes so long to move it macroscopic distances! The lifetime of the manifest universe may not be long enough.

So, we try thoughts and feeling, the internal stuff, the quantum stuff that changes so fast that we cannot even share them with others, have you noticed, between your thought and my thought, in that split second, the potentialities change so much! So, thoughts are private, they are experienced internally. That's what we go for?

But don't give up yet on the car! Ask, why do I want this car, this shiny new Ferrary? To feel successful, they are the symbol of success. But why do I want success? When people praise me, admire me, I feel happy.

See ultimately, what you seek is happiness, isn't it? Is a great car the best way to be happy?

In the nineteen eighties, a guru—a great lecturer and inspirer—by the name of Bhagwan Sri Rajneesh lived in Oregon, and he would be very happy if a disciple gave him a Rolls Royce. So, his rich disciples began to present him with Rolls and eventually he got about ninety Rolls. But then his disciples started doing unruly things of pleasure and the guru had to pay for their follies coming from pleasure seeking too; you cannot have one without the other. So, this guru ended up in jail for a night and was he unhappy? I (Amit) am not sure, but I think he went back to India after that, gave up his fleet of cars, took another name Osho, and started teaching transformation. I bet you he was being transformed himself on the job.

There are other ways to be happy than pleasure. Happiness is expansion of Consciousness; the molecules of pleasure just help prepare the room for it. You wait with those dopamine molecules in your brain, your Consciousness easily expands, and that's what you feel as happiness.

Imagine, you just got your Ferrari, you have dopamine in your brain, but before your Consciousness expands, another person drives in in a Lamborghini, one of those real sexy cars. Your Consciousness contracts! Your dopamine molecules so easily can come to naught.

The Essential Ritual

This then is the secret of how to intend. And now I can tell you the complete steps of intention making:

1. Wait for an inspired moment.

2. Make the intention as clearly as you can about your quantum possibilities and potentialities of life.

3. Make the intention for greater good; nothing better to put you in synch with the movement of Consciousness.

4. Now pray that your intention be in synch with the purposive movement of Consciousness.

5. Wait in silence for a discontinuous experience of intuition to come and guide you.

Repeat this way intention making whenever you feel the need. Like the red queen in the *Alice in Wonderland,* who thinks six impossible thoughts before breakfast. For you, don't dissipate, stay with one intention to fulfill until. …But six is just a number; make as many intentions as you need during the course of your transformational journey for manifesting the "impossibles" in your life, such as transformation, such as higher stations of happiness.

Invoke the archetypal connection if you are attracted to one. Sooner or later, you will get an intuition involving that archetype, intuition is how the archetypes speak to us; and then engage in the final two steps of manifestation:

6. Learn how to access creative Consciousness, that's the creative process.

7. Engage the creative process.

The third stage of the hero's journey proper—the stage of the creator—is crucially important part II of the science of manifestation. This requires much more detail about the whole subject of creativity which we discuss in the next chapter.

CHAPTER 7

The Secrets of Creativity and Transformation: A Special Edition for the Quantum Hero-Creator

To be a creator (fig. 8), to fulfil the third stage of the hero's journey, you need to know all about creativity. In the olden days, people had to approach this blindly, via intuition. The success rate was very low. With quantum science we can do better.

Figure 8. The Creator - Mahatma Gandhi created the nonviolence movement as a political weapon to fight the British

Our existing software as an adult defines the limits of our ego. Manifesting new stuff, new software for thinking is the objective of outer creativity; we use the new ideas for creating a useful product that serves the outer world. This in itself brings satisfaction in how we engage with our profession.

But this is not enough when we want to change the way we live, change from serving survival needs to serving higher needs. Living for higher needs is the objective of transformation, isn't it? As you acquire new software and make it part of your essence, your character, you have a new you, a new higher and happier station of self-identity as well, the soul.

In the olden days, this was the objective of education. However, only a few succeeded. The teachers, called gurus, an evocative word meaning uplifters, did their best. Nevertheless, even in a spiritual culture like India, gurus have worked on multitude of disciples through millennia but how many people have been transformed? Not enough in number to have much effect on the mainstream. More or less, the mainstream culture became quite moribund instead, quite like the dark ages of the West until science came.

A Brief History of Creativity

Science is an activity of outer activity with the purpose of discovering a body of knowledge that everyone can share and develop new applications to solve the pressing challenges of the environment. The application of science gives us technology.

The mainstream scientists try to sell the idea of the scientific method—produce many ideas by divergent rational thinking, then pare them down to one—convergence. Now subject that one idea to experimental verification and see if it works. If it doesn't, back to the drawing board.

However, it is hard to explain all scientific discoveries and inventions this way. Creativity researchers became interested in studying the geniuses in science like Newton, Darwin, and Einstein, or the discoverers of quantum mechanics Heisenberg and Schrödinger. What is their secret?

Study revealed something unexpected. You know traditionally, creativity, people think, is some endeavor that creative artists, poets, writers, and musicians engage in. The researchers discovered the artists' process when they do their creative thing via their studies. When they compared the process behind the act of great scientific discoveries of theories and inventions of technologies with that of the artists' creative process, surprise! The two processes were identical. Scientists are a creative bunch just like the artists.

I started looking at creativity in the nineteen eighties after I had my initial breakthrough that quantum physics is a physics of possibility for Consciousness to choose from. I also knew that choice can be discontinuous, quantum leaps. As a scientist, I already engaged in some minor cases of discovery before I took on the task of making sense of quantum physics. Not much quantum leaps there, although one event came close. But my discovery of Consciousness in quantum physics was certainly a quantum leap.

So, what became the burning question for me was, Is all creativity a quantum leap? Somehow a colleague in the education department heard about my musings in the university's gossip grapevine and invited me to give a talk there. After the talk, she said, "Yeah, you may be right; creative insights come as discontinuous events; people compare them with bolts of lightning. But can you explain the rest of the creative process?"

That is the first time, I heard of the creative process. "Whoa, whoa, slow down. What do you mean process?"

And this woman Nora Cohen says, "It is well documented. The discontinuous insight is not an isolated event but is a part of a protracted process with four stages."

Wow, I thought excitedly. Can the quantum science of Consciousness explain the entire creative process? That would be nice test of the theory.

Yes, it could, it did.

Classification of Creative Acts

Another thing struck me while I was working on creativity. You know, it is not only scientists and artists that talk about their event of insight as a sudden event; spiritual teachers, at least the Zen masters also talk about sudden enlightenment. Bingo! Is transformation the culmination of the creative process? I started calling spiritual transformation an act of inner creativity.

I became friends with an Israeli physicist around that time who was also a military man. You know Israelis; everyone has to work in the military except that this guy took his military duty seriously. One day he told me about his new idea of how they should train their soldiers. "See our big problem is to prepare for surprises. Our army generals prepare for surprise attacks in a situational way. But you know. Arabs don't always attack like that; sometimes they give us fundamental surprises for which you just cannot prepare in a situational contextual way."

Aha! I thought. A classification of creativity is necessary: situational and fundamental. Situational creativity is creativity within a given known context. For example, you develop a creative holistic technique for healing flu using systems theory. Then when a new virus, let's say COVID 19, comes along, and you invent a creative modification of your techniques, so it applies to the new virus. This is an example of situational creativity. The physical context changed, but not the archetypal which is the systems theory version of the archetype of wholeness in this case by the way.

On the other hand, we explore an archetype itself directly to explore its nature and embody that, the creativity required we call fundamental creativity. Fundamental creativity applied to COVID would require a quantum leap; we call this kind of healing quantum healing.

Creativity as a way to break from old ways of thinking as well as living is a relatively new concept on the horizon especially the way it is used now, very tilted toward outer experiences and products. In the olden days, people also talked about breaking from old ways which they called ignorance or unreal to the new which they called reality. Take me from the unreal to the real—*asato ma sat gamaya*—declares the Upanishads. But this was called *spiritual* awakening, not to be relevant for worldly people.

I began to suspect that the two processes may be two aspects of the same process, although my spiritual friends were resistant. When I had my own spiritual experience, I had no doubt; the process is the same, only the objective is different. Outer creativity is directed toward manifestation of outer products—a poem, a scientific law, a piece of sculpture. In contrast, spirituality is inner creativity with the objective of manifesting as product a "new me," a new station of homeostasis for the self-identity. And oh yes! It is important for worldly people as well.

The four-fold classification of creativity is shown in fig.9.

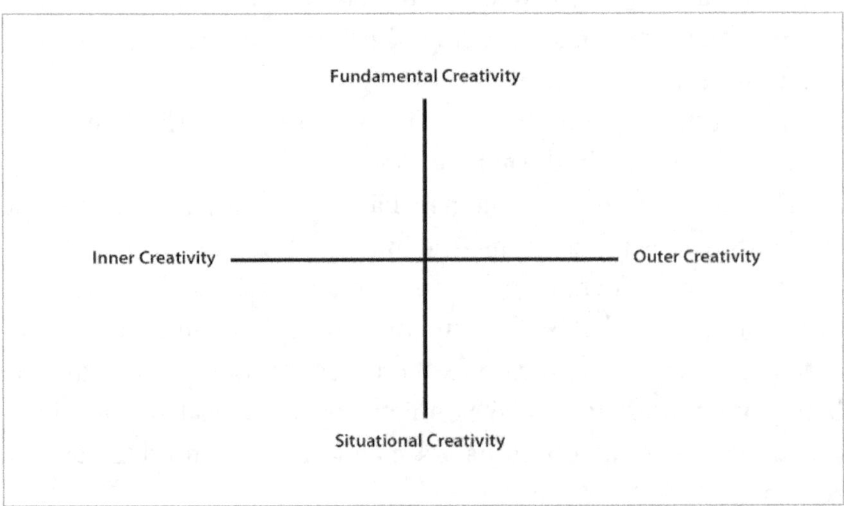

Figure 9. The Four types of creativity

The Creative Process

The creative process, as revealed by the researcher Graham Wallace as early as 1926, consists of four stages:

Preparation: do, do, do, think, think, think in divergent ways, use active imagination, visualize your solutions, open your mind to new stuff, think imaginatively and passionately.

Incubation: At the second step you relax. Here is how they got the clue that relaxing is important. Long time ago, there was a great scientist named Archimedes in Greece, who discovered the concept of buoyancy of fluids, the reason you feel lighter when immersed in water. The idea came to him not when he was thinking and sweating about the problem to solve, but when he was stepping into his bathtub full of water and the water overflew. He was ready as a result of unconscious processing during relaxation.

The same thing happened with another recent mathematician who discovered a new theorem of math while stepping on a bus for vacationing. There are many other similar cases. In arts, in music, in poetry and literature, in every field of creativity.

Sudden insight: this is the stage, just that split second, when the quantum leap takes place.

Manifestation: You got your insight; now use the insight to generate a product in the appropriate medium.

Do-be-do-be-do: Psychologists had soon figured out that what Wallas meant by incubation—the image of bird sitting on an egg—is a metaphor. When we do not process consciously, we must be processing nevertheless, but unconsciously. But this may be ok with psychoanalysts, how do explain incubation from a cognitive-behavioral materialist view? Sophistry began ideas like conscious brain action and unconscious brain action, never mind the anachronism of how that sounds.

When you use quantum physics for your thinking, it is easy to figure out what is happening here. When you consciously process, you are processing the manifest. As you stop, where do the thoughts go? Each of your thoughts acts like a pebble in the pond of the unmanifest—the unconscious and become waves of potentiality doing what waves do—expand. In this way, the expanding possibility waves created by you conscious thinking, soon make a huge pool of meaning possibilities to choose your next thought. Is that much better or what? Unconscious thinking or quantum thinking is allowing you (in your higher undivided Consciousness) to simultaneously process a whole bunch of possibilities. Whereas, in conscious thinking, you can only process one thought at a time.

When I became a physics instructor in USA in 1963, I remember a conversation I had with a very erudite senior physicist. I had a read an article the previous night claiming that scientific research may well involve creativity than just rational thinking. I kind of liked the sound of the word creativity, so I presented some of the ideas to this erudite guy as if they were my original ideas, impressing him no end.

Imagine my own surprise, when a few months later, I was struggling with a problem and the conventional known thinking was all blind alleys. Just when I was feeling sorry for myself, and went into the basement café (called snake pit by the way), and started relaxing with a cup of coffee, Wham-O. A new idea, the solution.

Much later, after figuring out how unconscious processing works, I was still not happy. Something kept bothering me—there is something more.

One night I was dreaming. In the dream, some stick figures came on a stage. Oh, were they active? Dancing, gamboling, jumping. That went on for quite a while. Then they went away. A voice said in the background, those are the angels of doing. Soon I saw another bunch of stick figures, but they were just quietly sitting, doing nothing. The voice said, those are the angels of being. Then those figures receded, and the doing angles came back. Then they went away, and the being angels returned, and it went on alternating like that. When I woke up, I found myself singing a Frank Sinatra jingle: do-be-do-be-do.

You know when and where I heard that jingle? In the fifties. In a song in which Sinatra starred called *From Here to Eternity*. The creative process must include many episodes of doing and being to get the result—insight.

We talked about the three I's before: inspiration, intuition, intuition; add to that a fourth I—imagination, you've got pretty much of what doing—conscious processing—involves. Imagination, of course, involves divergent thinking. You engage in these four I's for a while, then add the fifth I of incubation—doing nothing, just being which as explained before involves unconscious processing. Then a time comes when the processes converge; that is the quantum leap. It is a product of the unconscious, not of the conscious as creativity theorists first thought.

Manifestation: the Flow Experience

You know, you read the creativity research literature and people quote various creative people to make their point. Often, you find comments like, I don't write, the pen writes itself; or I don't paint, the brush does it, I just watch. My own careful monitoring of my own process revealed the explanation. The process these creatives are talking about is what psychologists call flow. manifestation stage. Ok, that's not an explanation, not yet. The explanation came to me upon reading these evocative lines from the poet Rabindranath Tagore:

> Melody seeks to fetter herself in rhythm.
> While the rhythm flows back to melody.
> Idea seeks the body in form,
> Form its freedom in the idea.
> The infinite seeks the touch of the finite,
> The finite its release in the infinite.
> What drama is this between creation and destruction—
> This ceaseless to and from between idea and form?

Our ideas come from the quantum self; our ego gives the idea its needed form. Creative manifestation is a flow between the quantum self and the ego.

We cannot create our own reality so long we hang on to just the ego mode for our operation. The creative choice does not happen from the contracted mode of the ego. Who am I then when that quantum leap happens? Who creates? Quantum self, who else?

For ages, that's what spiritual teachers have been telling us, that it is the quantum self—our deeper self—that creates. Ego is a barrier for transformation. So, we hear evocative slogans, "kill the ego," "die before you die." Is there validity in those slogans?

Slogans like that can scare people away. Are you prepared to leave the ego behind, kill the ego? Like the great St. Augustine, most of us would say, "Not yet."

Relax. If creativity just consisted of taking a quantum leap, then indeed it would be a leap to leave the ego behind. Realizing that creativity is a process of which the quantum leap is a part, solves our dilemma. Yes, we do jump to the quantum self when we get our creative idea or what we call insight. But all the stages of the creative process, the ego plays a role, sometimes an important role as in preparation. Sometimes a complementary role as in the flow experience

Let's examine the nature of the two selves in some detail.

The Quantum Self

The subjective state of Consciousness we experience in intuitive thoughts and feelings is not the ordinary ego but an exalted expanded state of Ananda that we call the quantum self to distinguish it from the ego we experience in our ordinary normal thoughts and feelings using our memory.

You can also think of the quantum self as the self of the present moment. It is easy to notice that your ego usually is either thinking of the past or imagining the future. If instead, you remind yourself to stay in the present and attempt to do it, a process that is called meditation, you will be surprised to find that often you feel relaxed, your Consciousness is expanded. How did that happen? Because you fell into the quantum self, into the present at some point.

Unfortunately, your brain, unless you train it via long hours of meditation do not stay there. Remember though that neuroscientists have confirmed that long term meditators do develop the state of frequent falling into the quantum self. Read the book *Altered Traits* by Daniel Goleman and Richard Davidson. But even a fifteen-minute bout of meditation can take you to the quantum self momentarily and even that brief encounter relaxes you.

The Quantum Science of the Ego

The normal state of Consciousness we experience is popularly called the ego. It seems to be quite predictable; it is certainly shaped by behavioral conditioning.

We also have the ability of being conscious of being conscious; we can look at the ego like any other object. Agreed, linguistically, when we look at the ego's "I," the I becomes "me," but it is hard to find a distinction between the two.

This confusion about the nature of our subjectivity has given rise to a mechanistic cognitive/behavioral explanation of Consciousness: assume that the brain is a computer that can cognize, that is, give meaning to its input stimuli that it senses through its sensory apparatus. The brain also makes memory of the external stimuli that includes the cognized meaning. It can process its memory like a computer.

In this way, when you are talking with a friend, although both of you speak in first person singular using the word I, how can you say that it is not just two brains talking, that something we call Consciousness is involved?

There is a way to tell. The cognitive behavioral picture got to be objective. If you both are looking at a rose, then your brain states must be identical. And yet, every human being "knows" that there is subjective quality of the experience that is individual.

So, to materialist scientists the question of Consciousness becomes a question of explaining the subjective quality, called qualia, of what we call experience.

As for the quantum self, cognitive behavioral materialist scientists just deny the existence of such exalted beings!

In quantum science, the problem is different. When Oneness splits in two, subject and object, when it looks through the brain and its tangled hierarchy of perception and memory apparatuses, the subject and object arise together, and there is no prior memory of it either if one is seeing an object for the first time. The experienced subject has no individuality of memory; in this way, it is cosmic, everyone has the same quantum-self experience. And the problem is to explain how during the course of living, the quantum self degenerates into the ego.

The explanation was given by the Buddhists long ago as dependent co-arising of the conditioned ego and the conditioned object of experience. Today, in quantum neuroscience we rephrase the explanation as "reflection in the mirror of memory." It is a little vague; fortunately, a mathematical model backs up what we vaguely can see and makes the picture credible. When all the nuances of the processing of memory is considered, we find that our ego consists of ego/character/habit patterns/persona.

Conditioning gives us habit patterns. Character refers to character traits—the easy-without-effort abilities of the ego. A musician can hear the scale a particular piece of music is using; he does not have to think.

How does a habit which you can take or leave become a character trait? Practice, practice, practice. Practice gives you mastery. Once in a while, you become so relaxed as you are practicing, you fall into your quantum self. Whenever that happens, you get a conviction. Habits of your conviction are your character traits.

We all develop multiple shades of ego behavior; each shade is called a personality. In each personality, we use a particular bunch of programs but not others; personalities are masks we wear in different situations. The ego uses different masks for its response to different situations.

It is important to emphasize the differentiation between habit patterns and character traits. Habit patterns are your propensities to use certain learned programs for responding to certain situations; character traits on the other hand are propensities that define you, that come into play easy without you making any effort; you have a conviction about them.

It is important to differentiate between your ego character and ego-persona as well. Ego character is authentic. Persona can be a fake, inauthentic, a self-image you project.

Neuroscience of the Self

To summarize the discussion so far, our conscious self exists in two modalities: the quantum self and the conditioned ego (fig. 10).

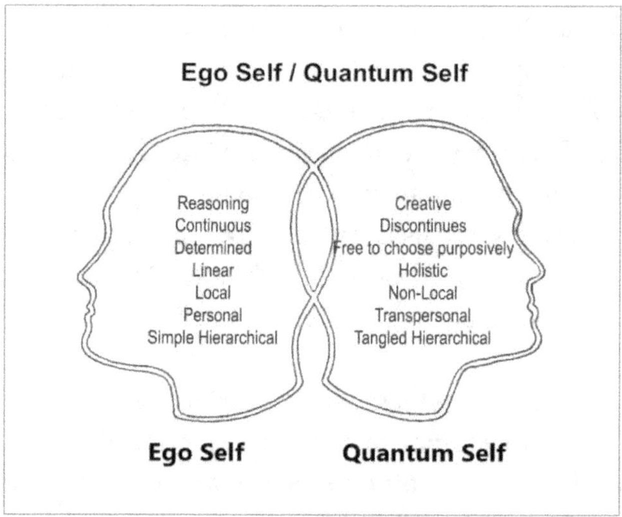

Figure 10. The principles under which the ego and the quantum self operate, are compared.

Neuroscientists have long discovered that there is indeed "reflection in the mirror of memory," a processing time of half a second between the arrival of an external stimulus and the ego experience, making room for the assertion that the experience of quantum self would be present-centered experience that spiritual exponents talk about.

The gap between the quantum self-experience and the ego experience is the preconscious. The existence of the preconscious has also been verified by neuroscientists. Meditation takes us into the preconscious and meditative experiences indeed become progressively numinous as we learn to penetrate the preconscious.

Recently, the fMRI technique has directly led to the verification of the nonlocal quantum mode of the self to be compared with the very local ego self. See chapter 4; also read: Goswami and Onisor, *The Quantum Brain*, for more details of all this.

Creative Motivation

Creativity begins with understanding—discovering new personal meaning of value about the information being presented. What is the value in that? Via understanding information in your own way, you are discovering your individual self, the potentiality of being an original someday. This is a very important part of creativity, strong sense of individuality.

What is the motivation initially? Partly, it is to aggrandize the individual. But it does not have to be negative, does not have to be motivated by the negative emotion of competition or domination. Instead, one can put the aspiration this way. If I don't investigate this, who will? Nobody is you, so nobody can investigate the way only you can.

Of course, if what you are looking for is more or less objective, then whoever is doing the investigation, the outcome is the more or less the same. But truly, the different paths to even the same outcome are often as revealing as the new truth of the outcome.

Partly, it is curiosity. As children, we are always curious. It is how that curiosity is allowed to express in a particular case that shapes the future of the child. Good parenting can easily to turn the child's curiosity into lifelong passion.

There is enormous social pressure to veer the curiosity toward the short term, toward the mundane things to satisfy our survival needs. Survival is such a difficult thing on this planet; it still remains the major preoccupation of the majority of people. So, it is easy to condition parents, even affluent parents, to behave this way.

A few children are allowed to engage their curiosity to the extramundane, to the long-term, and this number is increasing over the centuries. This is the saving Grace.

What makes a child curious about the "big picture?" Inspiration, frequent encounter with the quantum self. If this meets with specific talent—specific propensities brought from past life like musicality or artistry, or writing—the child is "on." Unfortunately, this happens not too often.

In the olden days, in many cultures, only those children, who fit broadly the label of artists, were allowed to be creative.

Other archetypal propensities are not so easy to recognize and encourage from early on unless a child finds a mentor. That too, has been rare. So, most of us plod along. Society does sometimes present challenges for the outer creative in us to show up in the pursuit of the professions, if there is a match, and there often is, the practice of profession may change the character as well, inner creativity. Again, the trick is not to be distracted by the survival needs too much. And name and fame.

But you know what! All initial engagements of outer creativity are just a practice for inner creativity from the bigger perspective of hero's journey in the creator stage. If you are into transformation anyway, a safe assumption is that you have done your share of outer creativity in your past incarnations.

Transition to Inner Creativity

Let's talk about inner creativity, using creativity for transformation. Here again, the question of motivation is most important. Such motivations are present (it seems by the quantum laws of our design) aplenty twice in our lifetime, the times recognized for rites of passage: teenage, and midlife. Midlife here can be anywhere between 35 and 65, and that, too, may be too conservative.

You hear a call: you are not fulfilling the meaning and purpose of your life. Currently, some teenagers are hearing it too late—because of over-addiction to information processing which really messes up the cortex and its functioning—they feel despair and commit suicide; the suicide rate for teenagers has reached all-time high. Fortunately, more and more young people are hearing it early enough to look for transformative education that would bring meaning and purpose back in their lives.

Social pressure is not easy to overcome. What is most relevant is that you get a second chance—the midlife call to reset your life. This is perhaps the biggest motivation we have today for creativity. Many people are not missing the call and that is why people, often highly successful people in the traditional way, are looking for "something else" that their higher education and career pursuit did not teach them—how to find meaning and purpose in life beyond survival.

It still helps to have suffering—mental or physical—as additional motivation. For non-career women, the suffering often is due to a divorce, due to children leaving home, death of a parent, or even when the dog dies. For men, dissatisfaction with career.

Midlife call for meaning takes us to our childhood memories to arouse the curiosity that we once had in the archetypes. A new intimate relationship can wake us up to the archetype of love, always a good entry point for transformation.

Lastly, activism, wanting to change the world and seeing the necessity of self-transformation in that pursuit can also be a motivator. This is a major one why we now have so many professionals in the pursuit of inner transformation.

Figure 11. The Ruler

Inner Creativity and The Middle Third of the Journey

The next three representations are of the creator engaged with 1) the archetype of power for which the image is of the Ruler or King (fig. 11); 2) the archetype of love for which the image is the Lover (fig. 12); and 3) the archetype of goodness for which the image is the Caregiver (fig. 13).

Notice that for the Ruler archetype, the power explored is power to survive based on survival needs; as the archetypes of love and/or goodness are joined, the exploration of the archetype of power becomes transpersonal.

Figure 12. The Lover

Figure 13. Care Giver – Mother Teresa

Difference between Outer and Inner Explorations of the Creator

The big difference is in how we approach the exploration of the archetypes, the middle part of the hero's journey.

For outer creativity with which you begin, you can just explore your dharma—find your bliss and follow it. For inner creativity as when you attempt to recover your soul, you must begin with the archetype of power; this is to reawaken your navel chakra-self. Then you continue the exploration of power along with either or both of the archetypes of love and goodness. This is to reawaken the self at the heart chakra. These are the three stages of the middle part of the hero's journey.

Although our ancestors missed it, the quantum hero should not stop the exploration here; he or she must re-awaken also the brow chakra with exploration of either truth, or justice, or wholeness, depending on your profession. Politicians should explore justice; media people and scientists, truth; people of healing profession wholeness, and so forth. Economists begin with the archetype of abundance, then power, then love and goodness, finally justice.

There is one other big difference between outer and inner creativity. Although sublimation of sexual energy does play an important role in all creativity, in general though outer creativity is more or less creativity of the mind. Inner creativity is by necessity, creativity of both vital and mental. Especially important is to work on anal retentivity (fear) and outgoing sexuality ("womanizing" and "manizing") and learn to sublimate the locked-up kundalini to release at the navel (courage, self-respect), at the heart (love, other love), and brow (to open the gate of intuition).

Transformation begins within known contexts of many previous explorers often well codified in the literature of "wisdom" tradition, that is the esoteric segment of religions. As the saying goes, a quote from Mahabharata, "the truth about that One (Dharma, Tao) is hidden in the cave, we have to follow the path charted by the great explorers." Be aware though! Good Books of the olden days were all written by disciples! Some good, some not so good.

Fortunately, there are books written by the savant in recent times: Aurobindo, Krishnamurthy, Dalai Lama, Franklin Merrell-Wolff. Of these Krishnamurthy and Merrell-Wolff can mislead you a bit, they were traditional, investigating only liberation. But are they good! Additionally, It is imperative that you use the guidance of quantum science.

Creativity within known context is situational creativity. How do you practice for it? How is it different from what spiritual teachers traditionally prescribe namely, meditation?

Meditation vs. Situational Creativity

In spiritual traditions, they prescribe two kinds of meditation, one for focusing training which helps to sustain imagination for long periods with intensity—concentration meditation or in Sanskrit *dharana*—the other is to train for relaxation or unconscious processing—awareness meditation or Sanskrit *Dhyana*. In Tibetan Buddhism, they train people to practice this with the archetype of loving kindness (another name for Goodness) in mind. The question is, how is this different from what we call situational creativity?

The meditators, too, also practice actual loving kindness with people. So, they, too, work on building positive emotional brain circuits.

And yet, the meditation traditions even today seldom emphasize the importance of discontinuity or quantum leaps or engaging the creative process as we currently formulate it.

These traditions also have the three initial I's: inspiration, they do Satsang (Sanskrit word for to be in company of holy people), they pray—intention setting, and they certainly know about the importance of intuition.

So again, what is the difference? We emphasize do-be-do-be-do; they emphasize prolonged meditation, like 2-3 hours every sitting and they carry on like that for years before achieving high levels of happiness. The emphasis is on meditating long hours.

In do-be-do-be-do, you engage in active imagination, maybe half an hour at a time, engage practice with people maybe a similar amount of time, engage in awareness meditation maybe again half an hour max. Your emphasis, however, is to develop a do-be-do-be-do lifestyle and taking the quantum leap. The quantum leap gives you conviction and character for the ability to call up your positive emotional brain circuits as and when they are needed in an easy-without effort way.

Meditation long time takes you deep into the preconscious. From there, it is easy to fall into the quantum self. And you feel joyful. But it is not like a quantum leap; you may not notice the aha surprise or have an insight. Except of course, any encounter with quantum self will give you conviction in what you are practicing, in this case loving kindness.

The result is the same: the archetypal response to a stimulus becomes part of your character within the context you are using.

But there is a big advantage in the quantum creativity approach in terms of time. The quantum approach requires more intensity, but much less time. The meditation approach requires less intensity overall, but much more overall time.

So, you use the method that suits you better. The olden day debate "Is enlightenment sudden or continuous?" is pointless. If you want to live in the world and serve the world, the quantum approach is for you. If on the other hand, you want a monastic life, then the traditions serve you adequately and quite satisfactorily.

A Few Things about the Quantum Method—Situational Creativity

1. The quantum method can be used for both healing and for positive growth. In other words, from lifting one from happiness level 1 to 2 and from level 2 to 3, but the

process would use different contexts and therefore, the active imaginations you use in the preparation stage are quite different.

2. How does unconscious processing work? In active imagination, we send many imaginary propositions and visualizations which then act as seeds for proliferation of possibilities via wave-like expansion. In unconscious processing, these possibility waves mix and interact producing new possibilities for Consciousness to choose from. And here is a big difference when you are dealing with level 1 person: he is more or less bound by his personal unconscious with little access to new possibilities. So the helper has to help with that, act as the uplifter.

3. In our hurry, initially, we find many pseudo-insights. How to discern the wheat from the chaff? A therapist or a guru is needed for most people both for healing and for personal growth.

4. If you include the vital dimension in healing, here is a big advantage. The vital is truthful to us. A feeling in the gut or in the heart is most revealing. It is amazing how easy it is to feign surprise with a thought until you have the real thing which comes with a gut feeling. Once you have the real experience of quantum leaping, from then on, it is hard to deceive yourself.

5. Resilience is an essential virtue for creativity. "Failures are the pillars of success."

6. Collaboration is good; having an intimate partner as a collaborator is great. Having a teacher is good.

7. For mental healing, manifestation consists of belief system change and change of lifestyle to include a new skill set; for positive mental health, you will have been using some

of these skills; now give them a chance to become per-fected with the added conviction and character.

SOUL RECOVERY NEEDS ONLY SITUATIONAL CREATIVITY

We cannot make direct memory of intuition; we do not have the required hardware. It follows that we cannot make a truly supra-mental body of supramental software with the hardware we have.

We can and do make memory of creative thoughts; this gives us soul software; we also make memory of creative feelings and thought together generating positive emotions in which both thoughts and feelings are used to make positive emotional brain circuits or soul software.

For soul recovery, the hero needs to use only situational creativ-ity; both vital and mental software are balanced between creativity and conditioning; positive emotional software is built to balance the negative enabling the hero to achieve emotional intelligence—level three of happiness.

The positive emotional software you made in early development is blocked by the physical-vital dosha called pitta and brain-mind dosha of hyperactivity; due to these doshas, the selves at the navel and the heart chakras become dormant. Removal of these doshas take vital creativity.

Vital creativity involves the same creative process as the mental. Instead of meditation, we use techniques of chi gong, tai chi, and pranayama (all involves a lot of visualization or active imagination). Relaxation or being consists of non-doing as before. Do-be-do-be-do then takes us to a convergence and quantum leap which is called kundalini awakening.

Kundalini awakening changes the feeling at the navel chakra from security to self-worth and the feeling at the heart chakra from defensiveness to love. If the archetype explored is love, then the love is romantic love; if goodness is explored, the love is altruistic love.

With mental meaning added, both explorations lead us to the ability of emotion management, the beginning of emotional intelligence.

Soul recovery and further situational creativity give the hero some soul software, but it is still ego's choice to make, to use soul software or not. To give up this choice is a major decision of the ego, a major step in the journey, and Campbell has emphasized it a whole lot.

STRATEGIES FOR THE JOURNEY-PERSON

This is the time to talk strategy, since the next stage—fundamental creativity—is so radically demanding. Indeed, the strategy depends a lot on your reincarnational maturity, your current situation, and what kind of professional challenge you will be facing.

Archetype wise, the hero's journey codified in our collective unconscious is about the transformation of people seeking power; however, it is virtually the same for people who are seeking abundance. Indeed, today, most people of in search of power also covet abundance.

The transformation so far gives one enough power for leadership in business and business management for which the ability for situational creativity and the software for emotion control are the major assets needed. Creativity, even situational, engaged properly can give one conviction in one's ideas, command in the field, and courage for new initiative. Emotion software gives us management ability of communication.

For people pursuing professions that require the exploration of the archetype of beauty, inner creativity at the situational level and growing software of abundance and power in conjunction with love is enough.

For a political career and leadership, the hero needs charisma. Ordinary charisma that our current leaders employ is a clever ability to manipulate others, push their buttons of inadequacy and demagogue them into followers. This kind of charisma is more appropriate for dictatorship. For the quantum leader in politics, quantum science dictates that the leader works within a democratic system now that he or she has learned how to empower others. But that ability does not necessarily translate into charisma.

The charisma needed is morality and the archetype of goodness beyond the good-evil duality of the collective unconscious and this needs fundamental creativity. However, the success in any exploration that requires fundamental creativity is unpredictable as to when; so. the strategy has to be to engage it on the job; to engage with commitment, however.

Mahatma Gandhi, Nelson Mandela, and Martin Luther King are recent leaders of such moral authority and charisma (never mind reports of their occasional failure in dealing with sexuality); so, we have relatively recent example to inspire. In the current political scene, it is almost completely lacking, giving us the crisis with democracy.

Obviously, for religious leaders as well, the charisma of moral authority is a must. Current examples are the Dalai Lama and Pope Francis.

For people pursuing professions of science and of media, the archetype of truth is the issue and needs to be explored at least at the inner situational level in order to stay upright under social pressure in the pursuers' expressions of outer creativity.

Pursuing on the job the archetype of wholeness with inner situational creativity, is all that is required for aspirants of the healing profession to enter the profession. The fundamental exploration of wholeness can proceed on the job.

For quantum educationists, people who want to initiate and teach hero's journey to professionals, the requirement is more stringent. They must successfully complete at least one archetype—it can be his or her dharma—with fundamental creativity.

Then they can begin to engage into integrating our three fundamental dichotomies and other archetypes to integrate their dichotomies as well. All this puts them in the exploration of the archetype of wholeness as well. Simultaneously, they can also begin direct exploration of the archetype of wholeness on the job.

THE THREE FUNDAMENTAL DICHOTOMIES

The existence of the three fundamental dichotomies is part of a puzzle to the children and parents should explain them as early as possible.

The quantum self-ego dichotomy puzzle is a big one. There is a true story of a 3-year-old little boy saying to his 2-year sister when she reported talking to God: "enjoy it while you can. I am already losing that capacity."

It is easy to dismiss such "child-talk," but that would be a mistake. It is quite easy to experience the expanded Consciousness of God-speak and discern its difference from the contracted Consciousness of ego-speak; we can do it even as an adult when we open to experiences of feelings in the body.

Parents, instead of suppressing such curiosity, really should clarify these issues so a child does not develop the misconception of a dualist God separate from us. They should find a way to explain to their children that the "God" they experience is real, that it is their inner self of expansion and inclusion, reflecting their inner beauty. And that all children have it.

How nice it would be if our children knew early that everyone has such inner beauty, that everyone is lovable, when these experiences are frequent. This would be so handy for their later development of moral concepts.

Creativity-conditioning dichotomy can be taught in an experiential way with engaging singing, poetry reciting, drawing, these can be fodder for pre-school activities. It is easy for children to experience and see for themselves how Consciousness expands when engaging in the arts and music due to their inner self participating in the process.

Children are often not aware about the differences between their inside world and the outside world; they need to be taught the difference between public and private, sharable, and not sharable experiences and the difference explained (one is physical, the other is non-physical). Their special nonlocal intimacy with mother and nobody else must also contribute to that excessive dependence on mother that some children develop. This is also part of their inner-outer puzzle. This, too, should be explained as early in a child's life as possible.

Boys are taught early on to engage in outer activities and extroversion. Introverts are discriminated against. Instead, parents should encourage a balanced approach.

This male-female software dichotomy is due to our faulty collective unconscious augmented by additional socio-cultural upbringing. At least the latter is easily avoided. Females should be encouraged to develop self-reliance as well as engage other love; males should engage in other love as well as self-reliance. Neither should be encouraged to build self-indulgence.

Maintaining male-female software dichotomy was at least somewhat appropriate in agricultural societies; and women reluctantly accepted their low social status then.

What changed between then and now? It is how we deal with power. So long as we identify power as physical strength, men have the upper hand. In fact, strong men have the upper hand. But as the balance of power shifted toward the mind, the attitude to what constitutes power changed with it.

Despite that, we had to wait till modern times and birth control technology to equate male-female social status more.

It is one of the lasting successes of civilization that we are finally civilized enough to try hard toward equalizing male-female social status. But we are still missing a clue.

Spiritual traditions have been telling us for a long time that power has to be explored along with the archetype of love in a civilized society. This is the missing clue. Until human culture everywhere acknowledges the power of positive emotions, especially love, equal status between male and female would not arrive in practice.

But again, equal status means nothing if women remain lacking in the self-reliance and self-worth and dependent on men for approval.

To eliminate the male-female software dichotomy in young children is one of the priorities of the paradigm shift in education. Not only creativity will have to be introduced in the grade school but also the idea of chakras and vital creativity.

Some Important Points to Remember about Fundamental Creativity

1) We cannot teach fundamental creativity. But science can teach some common methods used by everyone that succeeded.

2) A teacher is no longer needed to tell you if your surprise was genuine or fake; you are able to discern. However, a teacher can collaborate with you in your project of transformation.

3) Although it is true, that you can practice flow in music, dance, and arts by yourself. But practicing flow with a teacher is most revealing.

4) Although bridging the dichotomies are part of the wholeness archetype, but just as some self-exploration helps us with any archetype, similarly, bridging the three fundamental dichotomies is helpful even for situational, let alone fundamental creativity with any archetype.

Fundamental Creativity and further Soul Making

Soul-making with fundamental creativity begins with the journey in climbing the ladder of happiness after soul recovery and happiness level 3. It really takes off when we engage fundamental creativity to explore and embody an archetype. We end up with realizing the archetype of wholeness—quantum enlightenment. Hereon after, the journey never has to end; wholeness has no end.

This is the highest purpose of a human life: soul-making. No, not nirvana or moksha which liberates you from birth, death, rebirth cycle. Think about it. You have to take yourself really seriously to think that your worldly life is like living in a prison and you need to escape into nothingness.

Realize: you, we all, are just a vehicle for the Oneness to discover itself in manifestation. *Making it personal is the illusion.* So, the ultimate goal of soul-making is the kung-yin Bodhi-sattva vow: I will remain in this bodhisattva state (the state of quantum enlightenment) forever and ever, or until all beings are ready to be liberated, which is forever, because new beings will always be born).

One thing about the ladder of happiness. It is not really as linear as it sounds like. In other words, as we scale it, we continue to carry part of the old level behavior before we let go. One can be at a high level, but we should not be too surprised to see neurotic behavior in response to never worked-on stimuli.

Another mistake is to think that the archetype of the self plays no role in soul-making. The journey overall is a journey toward the quantum self, the same journey as the journey of self-realization. Quantum self is the doorway to all the archetypes except that when you enter through the doorway marked self, you end up in the realization that all this seeking was unnecessary, there is no self to seek. That is a tricky place to be. You, we, better be very mature before we handle it.

The journey of soul-making is a journey of creativity from A to Z. Further reading: Goswami and Pattani, *The Quantum Science of happiness*; Goswami and Onisor, *The Quantum Brain*; this last book gives the neuroscience details of the journey.

Commitment to Transformation

At some point of the journey, the question of commitment to the transformational aspect of the journey comes up. This crossing may require for us to face our fears, to step into the unknown with a lot of faith and trust. As a simple practice—ask yourself, what threshold is it time for me to cross, what do I want most? It is a simple question, but each will answer individually in his/her own way.

We all have thresholds; they are confining us to boundaries. With new power realized and embodied, and new perspective gained, we can cross such thresholds. Crossing limits—one wants to not be so shy to give a trivial example… everyone has something even those living at the survival level.

All heroes must ask—what decision have I been avoiding that can propel me into the adventure I am always asking for? What decision I have simply refused to take so far? I can cross the threshold but I'm scared; I am scared of what people would say, I am scared of burning bridges to the old ways, etc. Also, after we cross a threshold, *everything becomes tougher. Not equally for everyone but increase in the level of difficulty is* unavoidable. The ego doesn't want this adventure, it uses the drive of hylotropy to avoid it, postpone it; of course, the soul drive—holotropy demands it.

Which drive is stronger? If you are a hero, the soul is. But even so, the ego doesn't give up so easily.

For much of the journey, we leave the option to fall back to the ego, when the going gets tough. In the journey toward increasing happiness, we build the software for operating at the soul level but often reserve the choice to use it or not to use it.

Crossing the Threshold

At some point though, we are ready to make the commitment to a one-way journey. We become aware that if we go further, we cross a threshold and there is no turning back. We feel we cannot be the same person we were at the initial stage. Something radically would change in us.

With that empowerment, we can find enough strength and peace in the midst of fears to really go into completely unknown territory. Leaving behind the known. Sometimes, the hero/us in some situations have no choice. Other times we can bravely begin from our own initiative. Regardless of how we cross this threshold, we commit. And we do this knowing it will not be easy, and yet we are doing it. We also know that it is not possible to go back to life as it was before. Once again, a survival level example—you decide to break up with someone and be with a person you can't live without.

The hero's ordeal we are discussing now is the transition from living at both the ego level and the soul level to living exclusively at the soul level. The advantage is enormous; the journey of happiness becomes additionally a journey in intelligence. But face it: it is like DEATH AND REBIRTH. Now it's really happening. The most transformative moment.

The hero encounters a difficult lesson, enemy or a problem, and realizes there is no easy way out.

In the olden days, army generals were faced with this problem. The attacking enemy is coming from the other side of the river across a bridge. So, the general fights gallantly and pushes the enemy across the bridge. But as soon as the enemy disperses, his army tends to relax. Then the enemy regroups and fights and pushes the general across the bridge and the cycle begins again, in the reverse direction.

The breakthrough comes, when the general, after pushing the enemy across the bridge order that the bridge be burned. The only way a hero can do that is to uncover a very deep resource and believe in himself as he never did before.

Often, these heroes must put down some tools that they thought help them; even if they used them in the past, now they can't use them anymore. This is the final test. It is impossible as long as you still identify with the ego. No ego can pass this test. Up till now in the battle of life ego and its tools—negative emotion, me-centeredness and pleasure attachment—were a back-up to fight for the hero. But now only the soul can win the battle, this is the challenge. The challenge here can be a very acute internal struggle against our biggest fear. All our wisdom, all the soul software we have collected, all of them are needed now to make it through this ordeal.

The old identity—ego—must die along with the software that binds you to the ego in order for the superior homeostasis for the self—the soul—to come forth. This is transcendence of the ego for good.

The hero was caught in the play of the Sisyphus myth—carrying a boulder up a hill only for it to fall down again. The challenge is to give up the attachment to the boulder after reaching the pick. How does the hero do that? Only by passing through this death and resurrection… the ego will not be in command ever, and you will be resurrected as a superior self of the soul.

The battle is between you and your biggest fears, wounds, the proverbial dragon. Now the hero has to defeat the dragon. In order to be here and have this redemption and resurrection, the hero needs to get rid of beliefs of guilt or shame or other hidden emotions that clamors—you don't deserve that; ''don't you remember what you did to this person or that… how can you imagine you can be there?" that's one of the ongoing dialogs.

Consider an example: the Tibetan yogi Milarepa—he did a lot of bad things in his youth. But then he proved he was not defined by his mistakes. This led to his transformation.

Neither are we, the heroes defined by our past mistakes. At this juncture, we finally see that we are no longer defined by what we did wrong. Our mistakes can define our past, yes, but they don't have to define our present and they certainly should not define our future. It's like someone is saying to us—if you're still breathing, it means that God isn't finished with you yet, God is still working on this wonderful sculpture, still setting the captive free and creating the unique masterpiece that is you. Like a half-finished piece of art, we are not finished yet. But we will be finished someday as long as we don't quit. We may not like our present circumstances, but they may be the key to our integral spiritual transformation, the key to the real end of our journey.

Transforming Fear into Courage to Surrender or Unconditional Courage

Dealing with shame and guilt is the easy part. The mythical name for where our biggest threats and fears are present is THE SECRET CAVE. "Cave"—hidden part of our psyche, like the Jungian concept of the "shadow".

When the hero-we face all we fear most, we feel we are approaching a place of great danger. We are here to learn but the hard way. We learn that our anger, fears, aggression etc. must be abandoned, we need to get rid of them in order to keep growing; but of course, we can never get rid of the brain circuits! What a task.

We need to prove ourselves, to pass an exam. Until the exam, the teacher helped us, now we need to prove that we understood, we assimilated that wisdom. We are never alone, but now we need to decide for ourselves what we really want to do. We are forced to enter this inner cave. We have to uncover all our resources, strength, courage to confront these deepest fears we have. We know somehow that we will be tested, but now it's some tests that never came our way.

In many myths and legends and allegories, the cave is where "the dragon" lives, the embodiment of all our deepest fears and limitations. Unlike the majority of people who avoid facing their dragon as long as possible, the hero/you say yes to this journey.

Realize that the Cave is a metaphor for the hidden part of your psyche.

Entering the cave brings light onto your shadow. Now the hero in you realizes that the path is not like a highway, interstate with friendly signs to show exits and how to get here and there; now the hero/you need to orient yourself in this new landscape. More like being dropped into wilderness, you need to figure which way to go.

So be curious, let intuition guide you, and as you get a sense a direction, remaining open to what you see and hear. The path is not something you follow that is already there, but something you create as you go. How you chart your way through the woods may not be the same as another's. You are unique, your charted path is unique. In the beginning we all heroes may have the same techniques, principles, initiations etc. but your way of practicing has now become unique. The stages are the same. But how they unfold is different.

In order to sustain motivation—inspiration, intention and intuition—to go to the very end of the journey what you need now is a different kind of confidence. Not based on self-assertiveness, your navel self in command or control, no; in truth, you have zero control, you are lost in wild territory.

You need to develop the ability to feel doubt, to be uncertain and still to go forward—the capacity of facing opposites at the same time as the Greek God Janus does. This is more than self-confidence, it is basically what in spiritual parlance is called confidence in God. But this needs to be much more than unrealistic wishful thinking, a wrong attitude that has a name—spiritual bypass—oh, I don't have problems, let's smile. That would be just a cover.

Here at this stage, you become aware that most of your emotional problems are rooted in one deep spiritual problem: the lack of trust in God/movement of consciousness. It's this lack of trust that results in high levels of past tense guilt, present tense stress, and future tense anxiety. And if you succumb to it, this triple problem-producer will deplete every ounce of confidence, spiritual trust until you lose your sense of meaning and destiny and decide, "my life is meaningless".

The ordinary consciousness finds confidence in things they can control, but that is not confidence. Heroes behold! True confidence is not circumstantial, its providential. Often, we allow our circumstances to be between us and God, Consciousness. Real confidence puts God between us and our circumstances. Surrender, put your luggage down, you are already in the movement of consciousness! This is the confidence that has to grow!

Usually, people of ordinary consciousness want to control their circumstances, and eventually everybody's. They want to play God. But God—the movement of consciousness—calls us through such events that go under the metaphor of the dragon. Our control issues are trust issues. And for a better understanding, there is a spiritual meaning of power that is now revealed, that gives control where there is no control.

What is this power?

In the Bible, New Testament—there is clear distinction between 2 types of power: *dinamis* (Greek) is the ability to do things beyond your natural ability, you have *dinamis*, this is power, you can do what others cannot; the other side of power is called *exousia*— the ability to not do things you have the ability to do. To refrain from doing what you can do, but you refuse to do it, even to defend yourself, why? for a higher purpose. Anyone is impressed reading the Bible with Jesus' miraculous abilities. He made the sick walk, he made the mute talk, he healed the sick and raised the dead. But very few are impressed by his *exousia*. How can Jesus be a son of God—*avatara*—if he can be crucified, where is his power?

But it's not about what he could do that had the most impact. It's what he could have done but chose not to do. That changed everything. As Jesus was hanging on a cross, he said— "do you think I cannot call at my Father and He will not at once put at my disposal legions of angels? ": Jesus could have escaped his suffering and therefore aborted his mission of redemption for humanity with one call for angelic back up. A legion was in that time the largest unit in roman militaries, 6000 soldiers. But He refused to do that. Instead, he chose to exercise his power of *exousia*. He let people mock him, hit him, spit on him; he let them put a crown of thorns on his head. This is not just love, this is not just power. This is a spiritual side of power; not Newtonian power of force, but the quantum power of choice to do nothing.

It wasn't the power of force of the Roman empire and Jewish rulers that kept him on the cross, it was his choice and his *exousia*. This is a wonderful example for the stage of **resisting the temptation**. This is about integrity. Walking your talk.

Jesus' integrity made him to apparently—for a common person's point of view—miss the opportunity to save himself and just do what is good for him. Integrity used just to cut corners is not celebrated. Real integrity is almost like an endangered virtue. Real integrity is the moral power—moral authority—that holds all virtues together, the goal of all archetypal journeys. You will never fulfil the hero's journey without **integrity.**

No matter where you are now, integrity is another golden key for unlocking the meaning even in adversities. We need to refuse to compromise our integrity. Don't lie because others lie, don't cheat because the others cheat, don't get negative because the others get negative. Don't downgrade your integrity to the level of the people around you. Instead, try to upgrade, if possible, try to upgrade even the people around you. Integrity is based on a firm inner sense of values that allows you to stand your ground regardless of what you are doing or where you are.

Integrity helps us understand that outer or external power of force is an illusion. A convincing one but greater than that, is the integrity rooting us in spiritual confidence of surrendering to the movement of consciousness when the moment demands it. And then we the heroes are ready to move further. We have learnt our lesson, we've been in our inner dark and dangerous cave, and slain the dragon.

In terms of chakra psychology, there is vital creativity here, quantum leap at the navel chakra beyond the quantum leap that gives you self-worth. This is the quantum leap that converts fear of dragons into unconditional courage so that you can give up even your life for the sake of integrity.

TRANSFORMING ROMANTIC AND ALTRUISTIC LOVE TO UNCONDITIONAL LOVE

I (Amit) guess I should write a little about my own completion of hero's journey of the exploration of love with inner fundamental creativity, about how I got from romantic but me-centered love to other-centered unconditional love. After all, many people do what I was doing. They happily live in monogamy and explore tangled hierarchical love via conjugal relationship by trying to integrate the male-female dichotomy of the heart and the navel selves; it is not really such a big deal.

And indeed, the step from happy romance to one person to unconditional love where everyone becomes your family is full of subtleties. To me the subtlety of the journey revealed itself in three steps.

The spiritual teacher Ligia Dantes once told me something to the effect that I should try taking responsibility for other people. When it came to loving my love partner unconditionally, this is the first step I took.

I became more sensitive to how she was feeling when we interacted. It is not difficult for a human being to do that, in fact. Neuroscientists have discovered that we have some stuff in our brain called mirror neurons, some built in hardware. These neurons produce in us a tendency to behave the same way as another human being is behaving right in front of us. You have seen it on a crowded subway train; one person starts laughing, and everybody joins him in no time.

How did I lose this sensitivity that comes naturally? I was too intellectual, that's how. When I found my way back into feelings, this mirror neuron-caused sympathy came back to me. That helped. But what Ligia was asking me required one more crucial step, developing empathy. In sympathy you are just acting out an unconscious impulse. Empathy requires the ability of being in the other person's shoes.

Cognitive/behavioral psychologists claim that empathy is just one little step from sympathy: watch the body language of the other and learn to interpret it. This "theory of mind" gives you the ability to theorize about the other person's emotional state. They teach that in neurolinguistic programming training.

But this is still local. Real empathy requires nonlocality. Rational mind is always local and mechanical, but at the feeling level, we have the capacity for engaging nonlocally. Once you get a hang of it, it is not difficult.

Via empathic understanding, once you have a theory of the other person's emotional state, you can do a very quantum thing: you can set up the other person's thinking-feeling system as a filter to sort out responses to stimuli in your unconscious. You already have one such filter that sorts out things according to how *you* think-feel about stimuli. When you include the thoughts and feelings of your partner, in quantum physics lingo you have a double slit to process incoming stimuli in your unconscious (fig. 14).

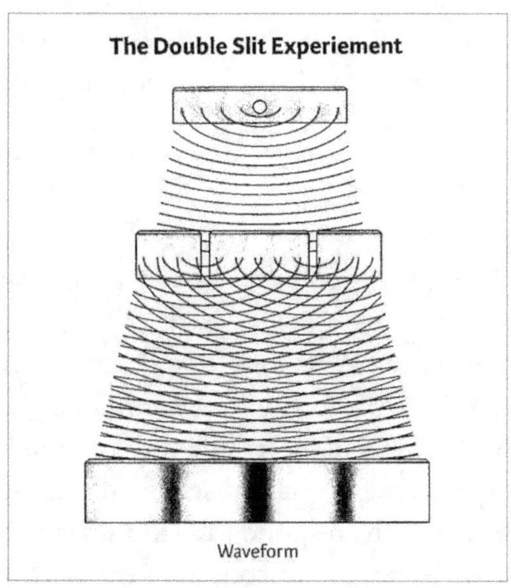

Figure 14. The double slit experiment

Quantum physics tells us that something wonderful happens when electrons go through a double slit and fall on a fluorescent screen beyond. Because it is a wave, each electron splits and goes through both slits simultaneously producing two waves that then "interfere." They mix in such a way that instead of falling in what would have been its assigned place right behind one slit or the other, it can fall in one of many different places on the fluorescent screen. So, if many electrons go through a double slit, they would make a wave interference pattern (fig. 15b), rather than a Newtonian particle pattern (fig. 15a).

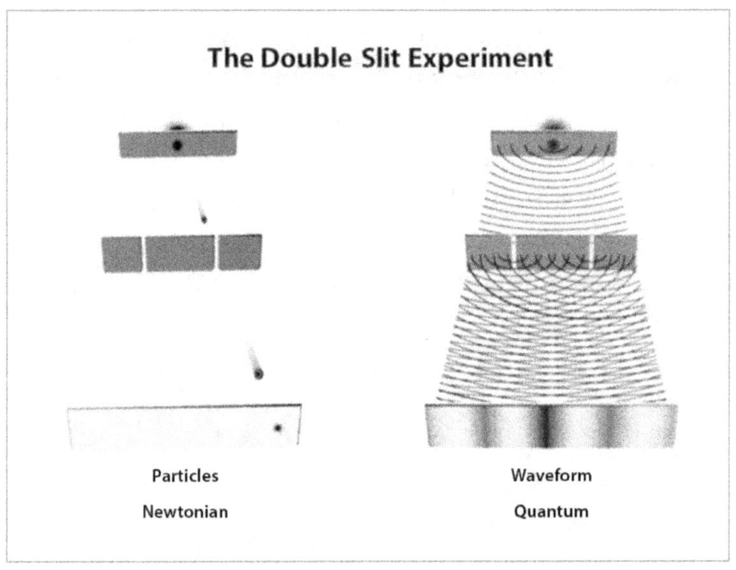

Figure 15a.   Figure 15b.

You see what I am getting at. By going double slit, you have increased the potentialities available to you to respond to a given stimulus.

Is there any other way of increasing the potentialities to choose from? Creativity researchers have discovered that there is. In conscious awareness, we can't respond to a stimulus in one way and its opposite way at once, but our unconscious can deal with opposites.

We love our intimate ones, but when our self-interest enters the picture and they oppose it, downright they become enemies, have you noticed? You love and you hate; of course, not in the same response in conscious awareness. But creativity theorists say, try to do it at the same time and relax. Let your unconscious process the juxtaposition love and hate at the same time!

Jesus advised something like this. "Love your enemy," he said. Pablo Picasso drew a picture of this, *the Minotaur,* (fig. 16), dagger and olive branch at the same time. The philosopher Hegel said the same thing, put thesis and antithesis together, and watch the synthesis grow in you.

Figure 16. The Minotaur by Pablo Picasso
(Artist's rendition)

It is so easy to talk, but how do I do this, posit to my unconscious love and hate at the same time? One time I was viciously arguing my case with my darling about the subject of our frequent disagreement, my/our excessive travel which her woman's body could not handle, when an idea struck me. I asked her for a bathroom break to which she nodded yes. I went to the toilet, closed the door, and took a deep breath, and started an exercise: to bring the energy to the heart. After a few minutes of that, I went back to the argument and joined in as intensely as I could while simultaneously maintaining love in my heart. We did not have a resolution then, but this was a very constructive battle of arguments. The unconscious liked what I did. While I was listening to her—being—in between my "doings," my unconscious was contributing new ideas.

Then finally, a few days later the insight came. It is one more quantum step further than empathy: to use sociologist Carol Gilligan's words, I discovered the "otherness" of the other and got my message. You got to respect your lover's otherness. And that's when your practice of tangled hierarchy becomes the case in the relationship.

What I didn't know is this. See, there is no making a brain circuit of an archetypal insight; no words will describe it fully either. Ultimately it is changing your character: to engage not in simple hierarchical relationship but in tangled hierarchical relationship. And live authentic to your character.

In all my relationships as adult, I had always put me first, the other, even a "loved" one was always secondary in how I valued the other. I saw through that now. Instead, Love is to respect the other unconditionally; then tangled hierarchy; then the other and I become one, a self, in which where I end and she begins becomes blurry. Our *local we* becomes a *nonlocal We*.

Back to manifestation. My lack of respect of my wife expressed itself maximally in my attempt to manipulate the wife and get my way so surreptitiously, even engaging white lies that she did not know for sure if I were not also maximizing her interest. As a result, she would grant me the benefit of doubt and give in. And become unhappy later.

And this giving in was really not suiting her. As I was getting old, and as she more and more could not comfortably accompany me because of her female physiology, her anxiety of me falling sick on the road went on increasing to the level of virtually neurosis. I decided to stop this manipulative behavior on my part. Serve her interest first. But it was very hard.

I would manipulate her, then recognize it, come back and confess, and begin again. This happened a few times.

Then one day, surprise of surprise. In the middle of a white manipulating lie, I became tongue-tied, I could not say it. I was amazed. I had lost the capacity of manipulation! I had burned my bridge back to the ego-level of defensive being.

So, this is how transformation works with things like that! God is in the details. From then on, other details were filled in as I related with my wife with open heart. Soon my transformation extended to relationship with other people as well. The new modus operandi does not take care of the *numero uno* as the old me would have liked, but it sure maximizes both people's happiness in a relationship. That's my story of how I learned unconditional love.

CHAPTER 8

The Heroes' Return To their Respective Professions

Hero's return refers to the re-entry into service to the society. The heroes are walking back now in the other direction, with a sense of triumph and a renewed sense of excitement and enthusiasm for life in general.

Not all heroes complete the whole journey before they return. Because of the incompleteness, in the road back some heroes need to evaluate how to return to life so they do not slip back into the way things used to be. The lesson to learn here is how to integrate sacred and mundane, how to put all new insights, skills, and wisdom together back into the ordinary world with service in mind.

You are not the same. But the world is the same, it didn't change at all, while you changed profoundly. After seizing your power, you need to continue your journey and help others, and keep the gained wisdom alive in the manifest world. It's about who you can help now and what you can do to empower them with your power—by doing this, assuming this noble responsibility to help others and even teach others as mentors or guides, because you know, you had the experience, and some maturity. And yet, this is just the beginning.

The last three Jungian archetypes in the list (see chapter 5) are about Hero's return but the return does not necessarily indicate that the hero has successfully negotiated the entire journey. In fact, more often than not heroes tend to quit after a stage that the hero *assumes* is the successful completion of the journey:

The Magician: The way our ancestors saw it, magicians (fig. 17) never complete the process of learning to share personal power;

instead, these people become enamored with just the creative insight of power and develop it further for their own gratification. In the manifestation stage of their insight, they develop so-called psychic powers for themselves (called *siddhi* in Sanskrit)—power of nonlocal communication such as clairvoyance which seem like magic to people. Today, of course, we call these people psychics. They do serve a purpose in society in that they bring awareness of ESP and nonlocal communication. This, however, is not the finish line and the hero will have to engage more stages; however, they can do that while on the job, while exploring the desired profession, when they are ready.

Figure 17. The Magician

With insights of quantum science, today we can encourage this strategy of simultaneously taking on the hero's journey of inner creativity and serving the desired profession with outer creativity especially for business and economics professionals—those in the exploration of the archetype of abundance along with goodness. The journey temporarily ends for these people after attaining what one can do with situational creativity, most importantly emotion control without suppressing.

We prescribe the same recipe for politicians with one caveat. For a few politicians who are ready, we encourage them to engage with the exploration of the archetype of goodness and love further with fundamental creativity so that they can develop charisma of moral authority. Again, this can be done on the job.

For teachers (of lower education) and healers likewise, we encourage the heroes to explore the archetype of wholeness and whatever that entails on the job.

For teachers of quantum higher education, it is necessary to successfully complete the exploration of one archetype at least with inner fundamental creativity. This can be done on the job.

The Jester: These are people (fig. 18) who have explored an archetype, achieved creative insight, may even have made some soul software appropriate for higher levels of happiness, but never bothered to complete the manifestation stage to get to develop transformation of character. They look at the world of innocent and everyman type of people with not a clue of what is in human potentiality with amusement and make fun of their situation and bring some relief to people that way from their often-miserable life of ignorance. However, this is not all. The Jester has a mischievous side as well (he is also called the Trickster for that reason) which he uses to wake up people from their ignorance. The legendary Sufi Mullah Nasruddin falls in this category.

A Nusruddin story to illustrate. Nasruddin is invited to a rich man's house for dinner. He appears in his usual shabby clothes and the gateman refuses to admit him. Nasruddin is forced to change to nice clothes; this time the gatekeep does not object. When he is served his dinner at the table, Nasruddin begins to put the food in the pocket of his shirt. The rich man inquires, "What are doing, mullah?"

Nasruddin gravely tells how he could not get in in his regular clothes and says, "Obviously it is the shirt that was invited. So I am feeding the shirt."

Figure 18. Mullah Nasiruddin the legendary Jester

Unfortunately, some of these people mistake their creative insight—gaining intellectual wisdom about an archetype—as the culmination of their exploration and become gurus. But since they do not (cannot) walk their talk, since they have not finished the journey's crucial manifestation stage, they often end up confusing their disciples.

The Sage: This is the mature Jungian archetype designating people (fig. 19) who have fully completed the journey—insight followed up by embodiment. Upon completion of this stage of Hero's return, these wise people become authentic teachers of archetypal wisdom; they are called *sadgurus* in Sanskrit. These are the people fully qualified to be teachers of quantum higher education.

Figure 19. The sage. The figure shown is that of Sri Aurobindo.

Self-development during Professional Engagements in the 'Magician' Stage

The hero magician when he is ready has a double opportunity: 1) to find a professional opening that would be conducive to outer exploration of the archetype and 2) resume the inner journey to find an institution for training in transformation education—quantum style.

The focus in this book is only on the three archetypes: abundance, power, and wholeness. For all three, quantum science has initiated a paradigm shift in the way these professions are conducted now. Needless to remind you that the current ways have given us crisis conditions.

THE QUANTUM SCIENCE AND THE HERO'S DEVELOPMENTAL POTENTIAL VIA TRYING TO IMPLEMENT IT IN SOCIAL SYSTEMS

In the hunter-gatherer era, beauty may have been the first archetype to break through the machine tendencies of the human ego, but the archetypes of prosperity (or abundance) and power could not be far behind. Given that survivability has been the primary drive for the evolution of life, this should not be too surprising. Even for lower animals, physical power, domination, and prosperity seem to go together.

However, until the humans developed the concept of individuality and private property, prosperity was not a personal value. In this way, we find large scale exploration of the archetype of abundance begin only with the advent of the era of the rational mind. This is perhaps why you don't find Jungian symbols of abundance in the collective unconscious developed much earlier.

It is the old story over again; human beings seem unable to manage without simple hierarchy and domination. *So long as elitism remains,* so long as ego's me-centeredness goes unabated there is going to be unequal distribution of material wealth and political power. Prosperity for everyone—all satisfying the American dream—will be pie in the sky for the lower rungs of society. And since power and prosperity have now been tied together, power, too, will belong only to the elite.

We need to deal with the quantum science of prosperity with this current reality as the context. The first question to ask is: where is the movement of Consciousness in all this?

Rational societies are difficult for creativity. Consciousness is self-aware through us; it exercises it causal power through us. It can bring creative transformational change in the society only through us. It is difficult for Oneness to connect with us with purposefulness without us cooperating.

There are signs of the movement of Consciousness within this broad outline of social development. In the eighteenth century, of necessity of dealing with impending crisis of economic misery and rampant elitism, human creativity cooperated with the purposive movement of conscious and created the three great social institutions of modern times: capitalism, democracy, and liberal education. That is the biggest idealist development of the modern era.

In the twentieth century, quantum physics was discovered. Ok, human folly took over and the movement of Consciousness was temporarily arrested by the intervention of the World War II. But after the war, among all the very noisy struggle between (materialist) science and (religious) spirituality, quantum science based on the primacy of consciousness was born.

But who will support it if people are still into their rational detachment from the movement of Consciousness? The same movement liberated women all over the world; sexism as we knew it, is finally a thing of the past. And women, long prevented from processing meaning by men, have a more or less universal need for keeping their heart open. It is almost impossible for a woman to give up completely on emotions. There you have the two prongs of transformation: quantum science and women's values. This is the way the purposive movement of Consciousness is taking shape today in the twenty-first century.

But of course, it is not us versus them, it is all of us. We cannot make societal change without men participating, without both men and women seeking truth with both facilities of feeling and thought combining into strong intention under the guidance of inspiration, intuition, and the archetypes.

Prosperity and Quantum Science: Quantum Economics

What is prosperity? Or abundance? Am I prosperous if I have a lot of money? How much money is enough? Why are billionaires not satisfied with all the money they have? Can we think of prosperity in other contexts than money? Have you noticed that just as people hoard money, others hoard ideas, they are very reluctant to share their ideas with others lest they be stolen? Can one be prosperous in vitality? Why do some people feel like they are vampires? Is it because they are poor in vital energy?

Capitalism was discovered at a time when the know-how was available only for material technology. No wonder, the discoverer Adam Smith discussed only material goods and services as the field of production consumption economy. The full power of Quantum science has been recognized only since 2015, when I (Amit) published the book *Quantum Economics*. I recognized that there is already a thriving market for mental meaning and spiritual values; this market is expanding via the recent surge of interest in mind and Consciousness expanding services such as the teaching of yoga and meditation, via the recent surge of interest in traveling lecturers bringing their meaningful and spiritual messages to fill in the gap in what the materialist higher education establishment teaches. I also recognized that health care is another market for subtle technology, this one for vital and mental. My breakthrough consisted of putting it all together and showing that such an extended quantum capitalism solves with some effort all the problems the current economic paradigm is having under the aegis of scientific materialism.

However, something added at the governmental level—monetary economics—is making things much more complicated and dangerous. A government organization called Fed in America controls the money supply. Crudely speaking, they can create new money by just printing it and keep the stock market at an artificially "healthy" level that way. The conventional wisdom is that this will produce inflation, maybe even deflation, simultaneous inflation, and recession. However, the fed can keep the interest rate low artificially as well, and so far, this tactic seems to be working.

As a result, all over the world, the so called "wealth of nations" that capitalism was designed for has become wealth borrowed from the future. Every nation is in debt; simultaneously, most individuals in rich nations are in debt as well. Nobody knows if this can be sustained or how long. But common-sense dictates that in the least this is an unstable situation.

The biggest accomplishment of quantum capitalism that I formulated and published in the book *Quantum Economics* in 2015 was to demonstrate, that an economy that includes a healthy amount of subtle economy—vital, mental, archetypal, and spiritual production and consumption—can be stable. I demonstrated that the invisible hands of the free market that Adam Smith speculated is actually the purposive movement of Consciousness. When we run our social systems in alignment with those invisible hands, our systems—economics, business, politics, health, education etc. progresses in synchrony with the purposive movement of Consciousness, they acquire proper balance of creativity and conditioning and become stable.

Economic Prosperity: Why Capitalism is Failing?

Suppose you have a piece of land in Texas where there are huge amounts of oil shales. You can make a lot of money by extracting the oil and selling it. How is it that this becomes profitable? Extracting shale oil involves a technology called fracking that leads to complete destruction of the ecosystem around it. The transportation of the oil requires new pipelines. The consumption of the oil dumps carbon dioxide in the environment already overloaded with that greenhouse gas. If you have to pay for all this, do a proper cost-benefit analysis your business would not be profitable. What allows your business to be profitable is help from the government. If oil is an essential commodity for the survival of the nation, and if it was a renewable resource, the government would be justified to encourage fracking. Right now, in the USA, this issue is completely politicized. The anti-environment pro-business party supports it, the pro-environment party opposes it.

Much of corporate business in the rich countries are profitable only because of this widespread use of deceitful cost-benefit analysis in collusion with the government. Take IT for example. It is now documented that overuse of information processing dumbs down our children. So, who pays to bring the children back to meaning and purpose enough to live a normal life in the pursuit of liberty and happiness?

Now look at it from a quantum science point of view. If you are into business because you enjoy it, then abundance is your archetype. Don't doubt it. If now you enter the hero's journey in the exploration of abundance, you must explore prosperity—amassing wealth—that brings that feeling of abundance. Otherwise, your business will just drag your happiness level down and money just cannot buy happiness that way—not caring for the community and environment. So, what is wealth? Wealth for you cannot be defined in just material terms anymore; wealth must include the concept of well-being as well.

You live in the quantum way, and your concept of self has expanded to include both your individual prosperity and the prosperity of the community. Certainly, making a lot of money will make you rich and materially prosperous. But ask yourself: do you feel abundance? Do you feel you have enough? Are you satisfied in an ongoing way so you can turn to other explorations of happiness?

How to make such business decision is to ask these and one other crucial question: Where is the movement of Consciousness in all this, where is that going?

There is no doubt about where the movement of Consciousness wants us to go. To explore our higher needs for the affluent segments of the society and bring the rest of the society up in affluence so they too, can join the rest of humanity in that pursuit.

Scientific materialism has done such a number on us! You would expect rich countries to have a larger proportion of its people in the affluent category, right? Wrong. It is no better than twenty percent, if that. The reason developing countries like Brazil and India are where humanity's hope is right now, is that these countries have caught up; it is about twenty percent affluent middle class in those countries too.

Anyway, as we have been maintaining all along, it is roughly about fifteen percent of people of the world that are ready and able right now to pursue quantum living and seek prosperity in the context of the archetype of abundance. If quantum activism can persuade a fraction of these people into practicing quantum capitalism, we can save capitalism.

A Brief History of Power

In the hunter-gatherer era, very soon after abundance, the archetype of power came into the scene. By its very nature, power and domination attracts abundance, but it does not have to be the other way around. So, initially, we find that in human societies the people of power denigrated those who explored abundance. There was a caste system, universally.

But something happened that threatened to break up the caste system. The story goes back to early civilization in India. In the Vedic culture, as soon as Oneness of Consciousness was discovered and the archetypal values were recognized, it was simultaneously recognized that the higher archetypes such as love, goodness, and wholeness, help transform people giving them a superior power, a kind of moral authority. India established a spiritual culture that respected the moral authority of the transformed people called brahmins that lasted for millennia. Brahmins via their moral authority were able to persuade people of power and material abundance to pay attention not only to their own wellbeing but also to the community's. When merchants transformed trying to share their wealth with the less fortunate and experienced true abundance; when the political power elite started using their power empowering others, there began a golden age of civilization in India that lasted for quite a while, millennia actually. Indian people still remembered those connected eras: they are called by Sanskrit words—*Satya, Treta, Dwapar yuga* respectively. Satya means truth, Oneness; yuga means era. This was the era when equality of everyone more or less prevailed.

It did not last. The declines happened in stages, called different yugas in the Indian culture: Satya to Treta to Dwapar. Eventually, though the social structure we see today everywhere came to be the case—*Kali* Yuga. Spiritual wisdom traditions degenerated to organized religions; the brahmins became the high priests of a religion—Brahminism.

The Indian culture has been the worst of the all the caste systems of the world because the system has become hereditary there. But make no mistake about it, the caste system is everywhere. In the West, brahmins in the form of meritocrats are a relatively recent fixture of the social stratification.

In India of ancient times, the high priests of religion colluded with the power elite of politics; the two together maintained a power sharing homeostasis. The elite of the merchant class were stationed as a close second. Then come the professionals, the talented people who explored the archetypes those times. And the lowest of the totem pole, the unskilled labor. They served everyone else.

During the time when the modernistic truce between science

and religion held, societies in Europe and America from the seventeenth to the mid-twentieth century, had done better. Scientific materialism grew out of the struggle between science and religion.

Did scientific materialism affect the traditional power sharing dynamic much? You bet it has. A new class has raised its head, the talented and gifted, the creative people; they became the new brahmins. Knowledge is power. The scientific materialists created meritocracy.

When scientists took the gambit of accepting an exclusive dogma—scientific materialism—that excludes religion, religions fought back. The old power elites of aristocracy and business sided with the religious oligarchy. This is the worldview polarization in politics you see today.

Let's go over this once more. In the sixteenth century, the wisdom *knowledge is power* came back except now knowledge was regarded as knowledge of the material laws that would take us to create technology. Knowledge of the science of how material laws did create technology and unprecedented material wealth. So long as science and religion divided their territory, the old elitism was not challenged. However, the forces that created scientific materialism also created influential higher education establishment and a society that needed sophisticated information technology that no one could do without. In this way, a new elite—meritocracy—came into the scene, a material version of the old idea of brahmins (and priests).

Science became scientific materialism as a result of a power struggle! Isn't that interesting?

Quantum Politics: Personal Growth Opportunity for a Political Career

There is a lot of debate today in America and elsewhere about the future of democracy in view of the rise of popularity of dictatorial leaders and their personality cults. The first question before us is, What does quantum science say, if anything, about political systems?

Easy to answer, you say? It sure would seem so. Quantum science disapproves of elitism; dictatorial systems are elitist whereas representative democracies do not have to be elitist.

This is not all though to the debate. The debate must include another political system: socialism. Socialism, like dictatorial democracies, is also elitist, it is an elitism of meritocracy which is only marginally better than dictatorial systems of autocracy—Aristocracy and plutocracy etc. Yes, democracy in a society polarized between meritocrats and autocrats, representative democracy tends to move toward socialism; this is happening now In America.

The real debate is not between democracy and autocracy; it is between socialism and autocracy. And here is the clincher: it is a choice between one side of sh-t versus the other side. Quantum Science does not back up either.

According to quantum science, in order to survive the attack from both tendencies, representative democracy in the current form is inadequate, it needs to be replaced by what we call *participatory democracy*. Its vision is simple: political leaders—the elected representatives—must use their power to empower the electorate. But this is easily said than done. It requires hero's journey and transformational education leading to leaders committed to develop moral authority.

Please appreciate the urgency of what we are saying. Realize how close we are in the USA to a dictatorial take-over when the president of the country has to defend democracy and publicly accuse the opposition party to be under the influence of a semi-fascist group. But such accusation lacks moral authority—why should people trust one party over the other?

Democracy, in order to survive, needs heroes; heroes to achieve creative ability, emotion control, and eventually moral authority. It is a huge opportunity for personal growth.

The good news is that at least quantum transformative education for leadership is now available as a modest beginning (read the epilog) and will go only one way—grow.

The Quantum Science of Wholeness:
Health, Education and Welfare

Let's start with health. Establishment allopathic medicine is materialist machine medicine. The basic assumption is: material hardware is all we are; it generates its own software following the same hardware laws. Taking care of it is no different than taking care of your car:

1. The technologies are disease centered: don't fix anything until it is broke is the motto;

2. The healers concentrate on fixing malfunctions, curing the symptoms via material interactions: cut, drug, burn. Cut is surgery, no complaints, an essential part of all healing systems. Drug is administering pharmaceutical drugs invented through empirical trial and errors. There is no theory behind any drug except germ theory for how antibiotics work against bacteria and (to some extent) against viruses. Burn is radiation therapy, applied to cancer treatment.

3. The care-givers—doctors and nurses—treat their patients as ignorant machines. The diagnosis mostly depends on mechanical measurements. Patients have little say.

Most drugs, even allopathic ones, come from plants. The organizing fields of form and function, those morphogenetic/liturgical fields, not only is used by Consciousness to evolve software during evolution but also to contribute to organ form, the hardware. In this way, plants and herbs should be useful for fixing both hardware and software, more the latter than the former. But in materialist allopathic medicine, only the molecular ingredients find their way into the drug. This is efficient when it works; but it affects the whole body, not just the diseased hardware of the affected organ. In this way, there are always side effects, often quite dangerous.

For car-care however, we have theories to tell us what defect means what, what the remedy is. It is really the lack of theory that makes allopathy disease centered; physicians don't know enough to tell us about health, health maintenance, or prevention of disease.

Except of course, hygiene which is tremendous discovery in the history of medicine. Also, allopathic doctors to their credit, do prescribe good nutrition and physical exercises for at least the physical body that helps disease-prevention.

There is also vaccine, but it is not an unmixed success. Controversy surrounds it: 1) the problem of immunity; 2) side effects. More recently, vaccines are using controversial techniques of genetic engineering creating further complications.

The most blatant failure of allopathy is for the treatment of chronic disease which especially are a recurring problem of older age; here is where a lack of theory hurts the most. People are put through dubious evidence-based procedures and pharmaceutical drugs of temporary cures that may or not prolong life. It certainly robs one the quality of life!

Finally, in the current culture there is strong pressure for making health care into a business inviting profit motive. This, combined with the banishment of the idea of absolute archetypal truth, has made pharmaceutical medicine a highly dangerous and gambling proposition.

You have to appraise the enormity of the development of a quantum science of medicine in this context and see your opportunity to grow on the job following it. Application of quantum science enables us to:

1. develop a complete science of medicine with both theory and empirical data to support it.

2. now that we have a theory of chronic disease, we can base medicine on the concept of health, we can make medicine into a preventive medicine. For this, you will need

to develop a nonlocal relationship with your clients and practice tangled hierarchy while relating with them.

3. Science of medicine now can include caring for both hardware and software and their harmonious working.

4. Health is the normal expression of the archetype of wholeness, it is wellbeing achieved by the balance and harmony in the working of all the parts individually and together—holistically. In this way, practicing quantum medicine is tantamount to exploring the archetype of wholeness.

5. Humans have five bodies; the quantum doctor helps her client to systems of nutrition and exercise for not just the material hardware but also all the different software—vital, mental, soul—and our connection to wholeness, too.

6. Individual caring of organ software means to work the conditioned and creative vital and mental potentialities with balance and harmony. You can help your client better if you are always at least one step ahead. This requires you to take your hero's journey seriously.

In practical terms, all quantum healers have also the enormous advantage having old health care systems for vital body care—the Indian system of Ayurveda, the Traditional Chinese Medicine, the Islamic medicine Yunani, and so forth. Homeopathy is a relatively recent addition to the list.

Quantum medicine is an integrative science that integrates the physical medicine allopathy, all the vital body medicine, mind-body medicine, soul and spiritual medicine under one paradigmatic umbrella.

However, Remember this: Only by exploring the hero's journey of transformation, can you expect to practice quantum healing with success and satisfaction.

The Quantum Science and Its Precursors of Well-being or Happiness

We come from the Oneness; we go back to the Oneness after making our individual contribution to the purposive evolutionary movement of Consciousness which is stored as an individual repository of quantum nonlocal memory. We stay in unconscious oneness until we are reborn.

What we contribute to the movement of consciousness in this life depends on how creative we are. If conditioning prevails, we waste our time with what Bhagavad Gita call *akarma* which can be translated as both nonaction and bad action. Quantum science fully agrees.

If on the other hand, we have the ability to engage creativity, then we contribute, according to quantum science. The Bhagavad Gita agrees, it calls this real action. How do we know that Bhagavad Gita is saying the same thing as quantum science? Because, says the Bhagavad Gita, (real) action is preceded by nonaction meaning unconscious processing, which exactly are what is recognized as intuition and creative insight in quantum science.

Modern Consciousness psychologists say the same thing—recall Grof's idea of hylotropy and holotropy.

Hylotropy makes us more and more forgetful of our Consciousness as we become more and more me-centered. Often, we fall prey to seeking excessive pleasure and develop addiction, a pathology; often the pleasure seeking gets mixed with negative emotional brain circuits and we develop various aberrations such as sadomasochism, megalomania, and sociopathy. In modern times, we must add to this excessive information processing and rationality. Combined with too much me-centeredness this may lead to dementia.

Not a good drive, that one—hylotropy—by itself, is it? Yet modern human beings seem to be following that destiny exclusively guided by materialist psychology. The other drive is holotropy taking us toward the whole. The two drives have to be integrated.

This is what a quantum healer has to do and this is one area where transformation is needed.

There are two periods of transitions in our lives, passages we go through during which we are especially reminded of the drive of holotropy. Many cultures have developed elaborate rites of passage as reminders of these important events of human life. The first occurs a little after the advent of sexuality, puberty, on the way from transition from childhood to young adulthood. The second occurs somewhere after one is supposed to be "over the hill," and descent (journey toward death) is supposed to begin. This one is often called mid-life transition.

Traditional cultures were based on religion; there was overemphasis on world negation. This is where the best of the elite went; they were supposed to have heard the call of holotropy early on. Rest of the elite explored the archetypes of abundance and power mostly guided by hylotropy as most people did not receive the privilege of archetypal education.

The Indian culture millennia ago recognized the midlife transition and prescribed that all capable people turn to holotropy when they heard the call of midlife transition and later gradually transition into old age and renunciate the world in preparation for death. Before then everyone devoted themselves to the archetype of abundance and power and fulfilled their intentions according to their dharma. This is how those ancient Indians produced lasting epochs of civilization.

Quantum science hints about these passages as mentioned above but not exactly the same way. Of course, we do have the two drives. We have the two selves. In the ego, we are more apt to hear the call of the outer—the material stimuli. In the quantum self, we are more apt to be aware of intuitions. But both are calling, always. We hear the ego easily. It is hearing the messages from Oneness involving the quantum self that becomes harder with the development of me-centeredness, especially with too much rationality and emphasis on information.

Let's go over the early development of soul one more time. Before the age of 5, the brain-mind brow chakra ego has not asserted itself. The child enjoys access to quantum self, pure feelings at the body chakras, and positive emotions. Agreed, the pure feelings are mostly experienced as memories of delayed collapse (collapse from choice now going backwards in time) at either the navel or the heart. Only occasionally, there is the experience of the quantum self in little bangs of intuition for which the brow chakra and one of the body chakras (usually navel for boys, heart for girls) become aroused.

At about age 5, the transition to autonomy takes place with a big bang, the experience of the awakening of the navel (for which boys are better prepared due to cultural conditioning). The awakening comes with important insights in various decision-makings that asserts the autonomy of the child.

Between age 12 and 19, a similar big bang occurs with the back to back awakening of the navel (for which boys are better prepared) and the heart (for which girls are better prepared) with the full insight into romance and awakening of the navel to finding the meaning and purpose of one's life.

The passages and transitions are real; in the transition to romance, we gain access to a new use of sexual energy (besides reproduction and pleasure), the exploration of love in intimate relationships.

In the transition from youth to adulthood, if a teenager discovers meaning and purpose, there is a possibility for another choice for the channeling of sexual energy, this time to the brow with the idea of exploring abstract archetypes—truth, justice, and wholeness—not only in outer activities but also for inner living.

Neither of the current worldviews gives us any reliable understanding of sexual energy. So, both groups approach the problem wrong and develop misleading sex-education making these transitions harder.

So, this is one area where quantum science is making a huge contribution. Happiness/well-being is expanded Consciousness; pleasure, especially sexual pleasure gives us a built-in entry to happiness, but it is transient, does not leave anything to build on. Channeling sexual energy to the exploration of archetypes is where the uniqueness of human beings shows up.

Although, the materialist approach to physical health is still from the negative side, disease-centered, the approach to mental health is changing. Positive psychology is a popular field in the cognitive-behavioral paradigm.

From Religions to Transpersonal Psychology to Quantum Science

There are exceptions, but on the whole religions have missed the boat on this one. In Christianity, the image of Jesus on the cross is how that religion sees life albeit they preach that Jesus already paid for your sin, you don't need to sit on the cross. Christian preachers do emphasize that there is peace and happiness in the afterlife, if one does not succumb to the evil. But of course, people, not bothered by the sin (it is paid for) engage in "sinful" pleasure.

Buddhism, in popular misunderstanding seems to be saying, life is suffering. Indeed, that was Buddha's first noble truth that he discovered. But of course, he was charting the course to follow for people with appropriate readiness for the final renunciation. For ordinary people, his and Buddhism's prescription is to seek satisfaction, happiness.

In Hinduism, Shankara's dictum, "the world is illusory" is for renunciates, not for laypeople. When blanketly applied, it creates misconception. And Hinduism as practiced is suffering oriented. The fact that the Upanishads declared that happiness can be reached simply by examining the nature of reality and removing ignorance about it (a process called *sukha-dukkha prakriya* in Sanskrit; *sukha* means happiness, *dukkha* stands for suffering, *prakriya* means *way*), is completely forgotten.

Progress in happiness thinking in modern times came from the work of two psychologists: the great Carl Jung and another great Abraham Maslow who along with Stan Grof and James Fadiman, founded the psych paradigm of transpersonal psychology with explicit acknowledgement of the two-self nature of human awareness.

The psychologist Sigmund Freud founded the psych paradigm of psychoanalysis based on his concept of the unconscious. Unconscious, he posited is the repository of all our suppressed and repressed emotions and is the source for human suffering. Psychoanalysis is centered on suffering. Jung realized that Freud was talking about the personal unconscious and looked for a source of creativity and happiness. He went partway and discovered the collective unconscious, humankind's species memory with both positive and negative archetypal representations, gods and goddess, angels, and demons. By invoking the positive symbols in our living, we can be happy.

Quantum science has perfected our understanding of the human unconscious with the addition of the idea of quantum unconscious—previously non-collapsed potentialities. Sure, remembering what is already in the memory is easy, but the creative process enables us to explore even the brand new, and therein lies the solution to the mysteries of manifesting happiness.

Maslow discovered the concepts of hierarchy of needs—lower and higher needs. He also gave us the first tentative scale of happiness. He divided people in three categories: the people of pathology (psychosis and neurosis), people of normal mental health, and people of positive mental health.

Quantum science tells us that are seven distinct levels of happiness (fig. 20), level 0 to level 6; each higher level can be reached from the adjacent lower one by making a quantum leap.

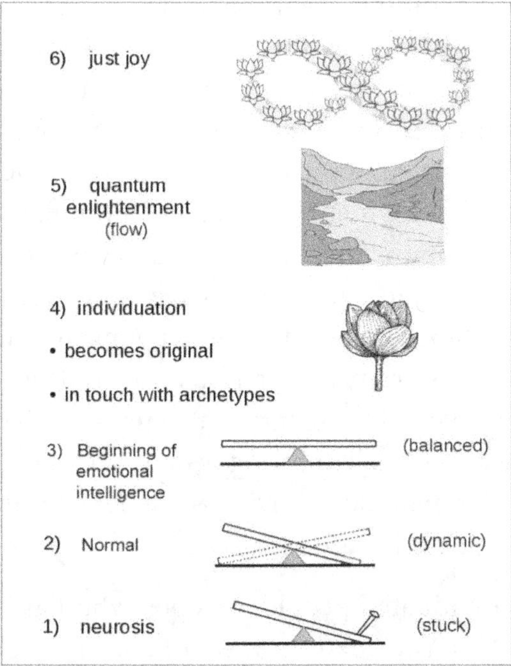

Figure 20. The Ladder of Happiness.

- **Level 0:** psychosis, creative living software in potentiality—yin—is completely blocked; no quantum self and no expansion of Consciousness. Psychopaths, sociopaths, schizophrenics fall into this category.

- **Level 1:** clinical neurosis, some cases of depression. There is opening for psychotherapy.

- **Level 2:** normal, healthy balance of living organs of yang and yin. This group is able to deal with normal challenges to mental health. Quantum science allows us to make a distinction of 2-, slightly subnormal and 2+ slightly above normal. The base-level human condition belongs to 2-; Maslow's positive mental health belongs to 2+. People of 2+ engages positive mental health practices such as yoga and meditation and have made some positive emotional brain circuits to balance the negative.

- **Level 3:** the beginning of emotional intelligence as part of one's character. In other words, this group has not only made positive emotional brain circuits but also has enough access to them for emotion control in some situations. It requires engaging situational creativity, a quantum leap of insight that when manifested leads to the development of positive emotional brain circuits needed for emotion control. As a result of this transformation, these people can do emotion management in most situations and relationships except intimate relationships. They can help people to elevate from 1, 2-, and 2 into 2+. This is the level of people most needed to maintain a civilized society. This is the level we are capable of educating people into but do not, cannot, even try under materialist version of higher education. We need quantum higher education for that.

- **Level 4:** Individuated people—people, who has made a quantum leap of transformation with at least one archetype using fundamental creativity charting their own individual path, the reason they are called individuated. Transformational education for this people becomes a collaboration with the teacher in an ideally tangled hierarchical relationship. This level signifies the beginning of a new level of intelligence that we call supramental intelligence. These people's emotional intelligence covers even intimate relationships.

- **Level 5.** Quantum enlightenment. These people have integrated all archetypal dichotomies as well as the fundamental dichotomies and have arrived at the embodiment of wholeness. As a result, they spend much of their time living in the joy of flow even in their service to the world.

Are there people of this level, worldly but more or less completely happy? Yes. The poet Rabindranath Tagore wrote:

> I slept and dreamt that life was joy
> I awoke and found that life was service

I served and woke to service was joy.

Realize: this describes level 5. And Tagore obviously lived at this level toward the end of his life.

- **Level 6.** This is the highest level of happiness. An extremely rarefied category of people who live mostly in *Nirvikalpa* (no separation) samadhi, a state of deep sleep in the quantum unconscious. This is popularly called God-realization.

Some philosophers of Vedanta claim that there is an even higher level of being. The position of quantum science is clear: we cannot verify such a happiness level, so we better not talk about it.

Can we verify each of the other levels of happiness? The neuroscience data is giving us a very hopeful affirmative answer.

We can tell you this. You know, the beauty of transformation to new levels of happiness is this: your reaction time to recover from the emotional upset caused by a negative stimulus, is drastically reduced so much so that you yourself will be able to tell.

This then is the goal of the quantum science of manifestation via hero's journey: scaling the ladder of happiness and later also a ladder of intelligence that leads one in addition to happiness to appropriate action. The teachers of Quantum Higher Education need to pursue along with scaling the happiness ladder also the ladder of Intelligence.

Happiness and intelligence: this is what transformative education as explored here is mostly about.

Let's explain the ladder of intelligence. You can be happy by just recovering your childhood soul and then coasting on that. You can develop additional soul-software in your journey of happiness, and don't change any further. But this is not intelligent. Intelligence is to develop the ability of appropriate action whenever the situation demands it, easy and without effort. This comes only when you transform who you are; when you develop character.

Imagine. IQ intelligence is mental/information-logical machine intelligence, level 0. When you climb from that minimal level 0 to the next level of conscious mental intelligence that includes understanding, you reach level 1 of intelligence. Creative intelligence is level 2. With emotional intelligence, another higher level, level 3 is reached. With supramental intelligence, the still higher level 4. There are still higher levels of intelligence beyond the scope of this book. Read our book *The Awakening of Intelligence*.

Isn't it worth to make your goal of higher education these high levels of happiness and intelligence?

Self-Development at the Stage of the Sage

There is not much scope of self-development at the stage of the Jestor except to go teach, through trials and tribulations, knowledge they can preach but not practice until the realization dawns about the importance of the manifestation stage of an archetypal exploration.

The last stage of the hero's journey culminating with becoming wise, a sage, is called according to legends and myths—THE RETURN WITH THE MAGICAL ELYXYR. The journey you undertook is *really* completed. You have stepped fully into your new personal reality, far superior than any previous homeostasis of your conscious self-identity; you now embody new soul-software and a new station for the self so you can live this new enchanted reality in the ordinary world. Now the world doesn't seem so ordinary as you thought before. Actually though, it is the same world, but you are transformed, you are seeing it through another lens.

In Shaivism, tantra, Vedanta, they say—there is a kind of distortion in what ordinary people experience especially those in the base-level condition; this is said to be the result of *maya*. The Sanskrit word Maya is translated as cosmic illusion like an act of magic, but it's prone to be misunderstood to mean that the world of experience is illusory, that it does not exist. It's not that this manifest world is not real. The world is real, but our way of perceiving the world as separate from us is not real.

Buddhism says—samsara and nirvana are not distinct realities, they are the same, it's up to your maturity which you can perceive.

So now that as a sage you have discovered in the ordinary world a new enchanted one, not mundane but fully sacred—full of light and wisdom, you can empower others into an initiation to recognize and continue successfully in their hero's journey. You can be an amazing mentor for others.

It is always good to remember while mentoring what Taoism says—the best time to plant a tree was 20 years ago; the second-best time is *right now*.

The Reward

If we succeed to keep our integrity and we have this inner redemption, a resurrection of a sort, we have defeated the inner dragon, slaying the dragon—then we are rewarded with a greater power. Seizing the sword (to slay the dragon) = seizing the greater power in us. Destroying our (earthly)limits gives us (heavenly) power and the confidence that no matter what comes on the path, we can handle it; we can surrender to the movement of consciousness.

In this way, the sage rises with a new power, fresh spiritual intuition and strength, a deeper wisdom and a very broad access of manifestation of possibilities. This reward can be felt in many ways, when you reach the stage you will know it for sure. It's impossible to not realize.

All that was so hard before, the three I's, creativity, emotion control, now come easily, and you feel relieved deeply and a deep state of peace appears, a deep sense of meaning and purpose of your life.

Maybe you're in a deep relation with your beloved. A new beginning, all depends on what kind of archetypal journey of fundamental creativity you took.

The reward is in some way the missing piece we needed in order to come back to the ordinary world from where we left. Our initiation is in some way completed. Now we can live our life amongst others but with that gift in our being.

Resurrection

You don't live in the ego anymore; you still have the old ego's software (except those that you gave up in course of the journey), but now it has been added to, it's more complete, it helps you to live in synchrony with your quantum worldview.

Realize! your whole being, its meaning and purpose is different now. And here is the thing: Even if you came back with triumph and ease, you need to stay alert, focused, keep an eye always open, to prevent any going back to the old tendencies dictated by your universal software of negative emotion and pleasure. It's like you have those weeds in the garden, it's hard to get rid of them unless you're constantly attentive, unless you learn to let go whenever you get in the throws of those circuits as soon as you are aware.

Now that you are transformed and know clearly that if you go back to the life you lived before in the uncontrolled throws of those circuits, it would be like momentarily dying.

On the other hand, you can't keep the wisdom just for yourself, because the wisdom will die. So, through your thought, words, deeds, activities, relationships, you have to fully embrace your homeostasis and the new reality. It's not about closing eyes and meditate and feel good and cope with the universal software away from the world so they don't get aroused. You need to integrate totally your awakened experience with the world at large, to make it valid under any conditions. Alone or in relationship.

We repeat: this archetypal hero's journey is not about escaping the everyday life or practicing for 1 hour; nor is it about transcending to a higher state and disassociate from the world; it's about falling in-love with life, trusting the possibilities, learning to ride the waves of ups and downs in daily life with skill and grace. To listen to and trust your inner voice of spiritual intuition that will continue to guide you. It has led you to discover who you really are, not an ego but a soul with balance and flow between the ego and quantum self. It will help you to propel your life beyond fears, fantasies, misperceptions.

In the quintessential step, you are invited to create an intimate relationship with the world and be in awe about your enthusiasm and creativity; simply being alive is now a celebration. Leave nothing out, dedicate your life to any experience sent in your way to embrace and learn from. Also, learn how to listen to the messages that life is sending you, both internally through insights, intuitions and externally through relationships.

Here we learn that basically all our journey is a journey towards freedom. We are not always free to do what we want; we are certainly not free to change our circumstances. But we are free to reframe our perspective. One of the most radical and courageous aspect of navigating in life is to access this inner freedom.

In tantra—freedom is seen as an inside job; it starts from the heart. Even when we sense we are trapped, imprisoned, we can step back a bit and respond wisely, and create a superior perspective. It is a practice that will not only help us but also enable us to share this freedom with others, as mentors, as teachers.

Humility

We declare again, the journey is not completed until a profound humility becomes part of your character. There are some mistakes that could be made, errors to tempt us etc. especially in the moment of victory we deeply need to cultivate humility, humbleness.

Napoleon, French emperor said: The most difficult moment in a battle is the moment when you win. And everyone was perplexed wondering why you can't just rejoice.

Napoleon was right; because at that time of victory, if you put down your weapons and relax, the enemy can regroup and hit you hard right there, being off guard. That happens when we are on a peak, we are victorious, we did it, we are up there. And it's a nice view, a peak of the mountain, we see far, we have perspective. But being on a peak—every step you make after that is always downwards, so this is the problem here. How to avoid going downhill. You would say, but that's impossible—you either stay on the peak or you fall down. There is another way. If being on the peak you keep your humility, then you don't take that as the ultimate peak or summit, because when you think this is the top of anything, yes, then you can only go downwards. If you realize this is just a step, I'm not at the end of the journey, not liberated yet, there are other archetypal journeys. With this attitude, you don't get confused, drunk by your success, you're not proud because of this success, you're humble. Humbleness puts you in a down position and then you can go up and up.

Humility is a key to fulfil our destiny. From a spiritual point of view. God (purposive movement of consciousness) does what It does and what we need to do is stay out of the way; how? by staying humble. Humility, just like humor—both words come from same Latin root, *humus* = earth (soil). (*Huma* in Romanian). Humus means to level yourself, to stay in the position of the earth, metaphorically speaking, not think of you so high, to realize that you're always lower than the sky, than God.

In China, the emperor was like God on earth. He was called—the lord of earth and the son of heaven. Because no matter how powerful he was and could do anything (it was a complete totalitarian state) but he always was humble towards the sky.

One dimension of humility is the ability to laugh at oneself. Proud people never laugh at themselves, they are very offended, angry if anyone makes fun of them. The happiest and holiest on the planet are those who laugh at themselves the most and it is *authentic* (the image of the laughing Buddha). The authenticity is important to stress considering this is the age of pretend behavior; leaders must learn self-deprecating humor as a necessity of the profession.

In the tantra tradition of Shaivism they say: if you have problem or are tempted by some demonic entities, try laughing at them, they will be offended and go away, they can't stay if they are not treated well.

Concluding Remarks

Time may be measured in minutes, but life is measured in moments and some moments are larger than life, and those defining moments dictate the way we see life. Some moments are predictable, promotion, graduation, marriage… others are unpredictable as an accident (a sign of systemic complexity) or a surprise (a signature of intuition and creativity). But we don't know which moment will become a major moment. Identifying them is the key to our life. Someone said it right: *Synchronicity is the poetry of our destiny.*

Each time you navigate through the hero's journey you have the opportunity to strengthen your resilience by discovering a new source of wisdom, and a deeper embodiment takes you toward a more mature soul.

All of us are in the midst of our own hero journey right now; most as innocents, some are in the everyman stage, some just started at the rebel stage, a few finished the journey partway and became a magician or a jester; and a rare few just got to the sage level the first time; a fewer still are already high in the ladder of intelligence. Truly understanding this reality will unlock new sources of power, love, resilience in ourselves. It is a journey of transformation for all; we all are invited to participate in the co-creation of the life we truly want. As we start working with the insight and inspiration, as we cultivate resilience, as we will learn to appreciate as many moments as possible, we make progress. We discover new levels of authenticity as we align all components of our being and integrate everything.

Finally, You the reader need to appreciate the following as a constant reminder:

- There are no quick fixes!

- You are not competing with anyone. Every path ends as a unique path, you need to follow your own destiny.

- In the Bhagavat Gita—Krishna says to Arjuna—do not copy someone else s dharma, it's not yours, it can be even dangerous. Quantum science fully agrees. You need to live according to your own dharma, purpose, journey.

- The ego doesn't need to die (that would be bad for creativity)—ego is a very useful instrument. Just that it doesn't have to create barriers; it does not have to be the boss. We need to purify it and put it at its place, then it's perfect.

- Slaying the dragon means to transform, integrate.

CHAPTER 9

Cancelling Education that Allows Dumb and Dumber: How Quantum Lower Education and Quantum Educators Can Empower Young People

In America and in more or less the whole world, there are now two entire generations who have grown up in the so-called information age. Thoughts are no longer seen by the academe (everywhere) as expressions of meaning processing because only information is claimed to be real. For the manifest external world, only what we can see outside of us and can form a consensus about is considered real. For the mental, only what can be computed is considered real. Meaning cannot be computed, so it is not real.

Ironically, this is a message for the masses. The elite of course does the opposite. Today, it is hard to get raw facts (information) without commentary (spin with prejudiced meaning) which the pundits provide. But of course, the meanings are old hash of old meanings; this is why the big excitement about new computer programs that can write student term papers and commentators' op-ed.

In this way, what the masses are getting as information is actually other people's (the elite that now includes the media) mechanically cultivated meaning. The elite in America are divided in two camps—progressives (sometimes called liberal) and reactionaries (sometimes called conservatives)—both struggling for power. The information they feed people use different data base to feed people misinformation or incomplete dogmatic information and create two polarized groups living in different tents who cannot communicate: the lower-educated who live in the reactionary tent and the higher educated who live in the progressive tent.

Reminder: How the Tents were Created

It is useful to go over the creation of the tents once more. Let's be explicit about the difference between progressives and reactionaries and also their previous nomenclature—liberals and conservative. Originally, liberals were literally the avant-garde bringing in new ideas to implement, ideas that generally took the three bastions of modernism forward—capitalism, democracy, and liberal education. They favored the redistribution of capital creating more middle class and were against elitism of any kind; they supported more participatory democracy, they favored dogma-free education to liberate people from the shackles of ignorance. However, the solutions liberal favored often led to bigger and bigger government. The conservatives were not against the liberal agenda; they were just conservative. They did not like the idea of big government solving problems for people because that takes people's incentives away. They did not support rapid pace for social change either. Such changes are superficial; lasting serious changes take time.

Generally, the liberals wanted rapid progress and relied on science and technology to bring rapid change. Their support of science and technology was blind; the politicians hardly noticed or cared when scientists adopted the dogma of materialism. They tacitly went along with it at the same time continuing to profess their religious beliefs in God and spiritual values.

When religious groups in the USA started regrouping against materialism and proclaimed moral majority to assert their political muscle, the conservatives saw an opportunity and adapted the new reactionary Christian movement and aligned themselves with them.

In the thirties, there was the great depression. The liberals claimed to have pulled America out of it by instituting what is called demand side economics; increase demand by creating government infrastructure projects and social safety net in this way putting income in people's hands. In the nineteen eighties, the conservatives founded supply side economics: there was a recession; they found the reactionary answer to the liberals' demand side solution to recession: cut taxes for the rich. The extra money will trickle down to the people and economy will expand.

As this reactionary approach seemed to work much better than the old-fashioned conservatism in the march towards more power, gradually, the conservative movement morphed into the reactionary motto to whatever the opposition proposed. If the opposition was supporting materialist science, they would be anti-science even to the extent of opposing the idea of evolution in spite of the compelling fossil data.

As the progressives sank deeper and deeper into materialism, some liberal thinkers recognized the problem science was raising—no spiritual values. But of course, giving up on values is not popular, not good politics; so quickly they adapted the existential/humanist policy: values are part of being human; they are human created values. We don't necessarily need to change our permissive lifestyle for the sake of values, but we must at least pretend to behave according to these human values.

The reactionaries found a legitimate issue: many people do not like pretension. Their answer was to let it all hang out. They became the party of racists, white supremacists, sexists, homophobes, quite openly. Many people prefer religious values and oppose materialist science. The reactionaries stoke the anti-science sentiment as well.

As meaning and purposive values were banished, social systems based on legality became complex and full of loopholes that the elite could take advantage of; furthermore, higher education became job training for dealing with the complexity, artificially created though it was.

Finally, what broke the camel's back was: 1) the complexity of materialist approaches to not only science but also to social sciences, and even humanities became overwhelming, 2) the cost of college education went skyrocketing partly because of the administrative costs of enforcing pretend values, and 3) it took increasing amounts of time to get higher education, 4) getting higher education was no longer a guarantee for high paying jobs. Many people just could not see any value of going to college.

The reactionaries and their media saw another opportunity and quickly manipulated themselves as the bastion of the lower educated ordinary people. On the other hand, the progressives remained steadfast in their support of materialist science and the complex legality-based society it led to. They, too, were to manipulate capable youngsters mired with excess intellectualism by catering to their ambition. Thus was created the lower educated-higher educated split.

To remind you once again: The elitism of the progressives is meritocracy; the reactionary elitism is old-fashioned aristocracy and plutocracy—elitism of the reactionary rich.

What liberals did not count on is how quickly the labor—once the bulk of their support—became realigned with the reactionaries charmed by the manipulative charisma of the leaders of the reactionary movement. This is because, the elitism of aristocracy is supported by the software that our ancestors created called the collective unconscious—the Jungian archetype of power is the ruler, the image is that of a king.

Similarly, our ancestors codified the 'white is beautiful, black is dangerous and ugly' archetypal images in humanity's collective unconscious that support racism. In this way, reactionary ideas quickly resonated with the lower-educated people defying the prevalent political common sense.

On top of this polarization, take special notice that there is vested interest in both groups to maintain the polarization, not to solve it. In this way the progressives go on bestowing student loan forgiveness and promoting free college education which is a privilege, not a right (since in the current situation of prevailing elitism, many students are simply not ready for college education). Imagine that! Free job training: who would not be obliged after a gift like that? And manipulated. But the students who receive gifts like this will never learn responsibility.

The reactionaries go on promoting hate focusing on immigrants, never mind that immigration is a strong suit for any country; especially for the USA, immigration has always been a bright harbinger of creativity and new ideas. The kids suffer; growing up in hateful environment they become narcissistic, learning impaired.

As Abraham Lincoln said, a divided house cannot stand. A big challenge of quantum education for grade school is to reduce, even eliminate the split of lower educated and higher educated people.

How the Lower Educated-Higher Educated Divide is Created: more Details

In the past, people of lower economic class grew their children to aspire for social mobility; to move higher up in the totem pole to middle class, you have to get education, first school, then college; they instilled this course of things in their kids before the kids started grade school and continued doing so. Kids saw their parents making sacrifices for their upward mobility; this gave them added motivation.

As we previously discussed, there are two crucial periods of child development: 1) the age 5-7 when children learn personal autonomy; and 2) age 12-19 when students learn to deal with the awakening of sexuality on one hand and meaning and purpose on the other hand. However, for children growing up in this information age, new challenges have arisen, making things complicated.

Three factors contribute to child development: nature, nurture, and reincarnation. Nature contributes the genes that helps build the hardware; nurture and reincarnation contribute software.

Much of the software is personal. However, part of the software is universal codified as nonlocal memory in our collective unconscious. Our ancestors, acting collectively, built this for us.

Our mental memory-making apparatus is not fully ready until about age 5. Naturally, this is when kids start to develop autonomy instead of depending on parents. This operationally means that children are ready to assert the causal power of their developing a mental ego in choosing their own affairs.

Materialists see this as a transition from no individual mental ego (Piaget called this pre-operational ego) to an individual mental ago—autonomy. In quantum science we see this differently.

When a child is born, the mental memory making capacity is not built yet, that takes about a year. How does a new-born cognize then? It cognizes with the help of a self at the mid-brain that we share with mammals; additionally, the selves in the body, at the navel and at the heart chakra, also help the child to cognize.

As the mental memory-making capacity develops, the mind starts adding thoughts to feeling making them into emotions. Since the body selves are also very much a contributing factor, the emotions experienced by children are not particularly dominated by the negative emotional circuits in the mid-brain; there is also much positivity, since nonlocality, intuitions and quantum self also play a significant role in child development in that very early age of 1-5. In fact, as the mind develops, the mid-brain self, more and more is replaced by the cortical self in terms of stimulus-response and is soon relegated to the unconscious. The negative emotional circuits then become virtually unconscious in terms of immediate response until the cortex enters the action. The conscious in the brain is dominated by the cortical self.

In the body, however, kids still have awareness at the navel and the heart with another twist. Historically in the past, we have always lived in male-dominated societies—more or less. Little girls were traditionally told to pay attention to other love (after all, they have to be mothers when they grow up, that would be their main job!). Little boys on the other hand were told to be independent.

In terms of the selves in the body what this translates into is that girls learn to develop their heart-self software, boys their navel-self software creating what is called the beginning of male-female dichotomy. The navel self-software is base-level however—self-indulgent and narcissistic. Because this is built into the collective unconscious, and kids live much of their time in quantum self with access to collective unconscious, even today, this behavior develops automatically unless parents actively intervene.

Now let's go back to age 5 and autonomy. In quantum science we see this as an opportunity for a quantum leap at the navel: the result is self-worth. Kids with adequate reincarnational maturity easily take the quantum leap and develop self-worth; but kids with not much reincarnational history miss the quantum leap and remain mired in narcissistic tendencies.

When we take account of the male-female dichotomy, here the males have an advantage having already some access to navel self and its software; in this way most male kids with reincarnational maturity make this transition easily. Girls may not be so fortunate.

In this way, male kids now with a feeling of self-worth make room for the cortical ego as well. Either can dominate and the data of human personality development classification in terms of enneagrams confirm this.

Females, however, are conditioned not to pay attention to navel self-software. Girls who succumb to the socio-cultural traditional conditioning do not take a quantum leap, do not develop a strong navel self, do not develop autonomy. As socially desired in male-dominated societies, they become dependent on the males for support.

The kids unable to make the quantum leap of self-worth will be shortchanged in developing the intellectual software necessary for later success in life as well.

In the current information-dominated culture, things have changed even further. Even before little boys reach the age of 5, they will have access to cell phone and social media and are encouraged to use them (since their parents use them too and the society generally approves it) even to the extent of being addicted.

Many psychologists have pointed out that kids become dumb and dumber this way, they never get access to meaning, they never develop a sense of purpose other than the built-in survival needs. Their ambitions never rise beyond the American dream of good car, good house, sexy spouse. In other words, these males and females in the future will comfortably settle down in the base-level human condition. They will be very comfortable with what a materialist life-style offers: eat, drink, be merry, entertain yourself. Naturally, they will be resistant to the complexity of materialist higher education.

In this way, currently, perhaps a high percentage of the future adult population—both girls and boys—is being shortchanged.

There is more. What happens at puberty with sexuality is also crucial. Again, the question is how to deal with the emerging sexuality. There is some instinct for romantic love available in the collective unconscious, but there is an entrance requirement; one has to lower one's defensiveness to take a quantum leap to a higher physiology at the heart chakra. Kids have a choice. If they give up defensiveness and allow vulnerability in their interactions with the opposite sex, they can make the quantum leap that wakes up their heart-self to romantic love; otherwise not. They will remain dominated by the immune defensiveness at the heart.

Here females have the advantage. Because they already have been conditioned for at least altruistic other love, a transition to a quantum heart and romantic love is easier for them. This does not make up for poor autonomy due to a weak navel self but gives them something to combat excess rationality. The male-female brain difference of hardware also helps here: males can suppress emotions and do and can keep quiet about their inner emotions; females are unable to suppress emotions; they also talk too much to keep themselves aloof; this is good for relationship but not good for autonomy. Read our book, *The Quantum Brain*

Males are really shortchanged for the exploration of love in the current information culture as part of which teens have unbridled access to hard-core pornography that presents a very materialist view of sexuality as casual entertainment. Some social commentary on this has begun, but they usually miss the point.

The point is this. If the heart does not awaken, the excess sexual energy sublimates to the navel to collapse; and boys become ever more narcissistic as a result; they become users of sexuality, they see sex as conquesting, not as lovemaking. Later these men become women abusers.

Now do you see what the current information dominated culture is doing, has done already? The first, by not waking up the navel self, many people of both sexes today develop dependency. Males are able to hide it successfully by projecting superiority: white supremacy, racism, sexism and all that. Females, being dependent on these males, even though woke to the heart, are easily dominated by the males, and manipulated by them into the hate-dominated behavior.

Weak navel chakra is what makes these people vulnerable to political manipulations by dictatorial leaders who know how to push their buttons. In this way, these people constitute the tent of the non-college educated group dominated by charismatic male (a few females as well) leaders.

Even people who managed to awaken their navel chakra have problems, especially males, due to their un-awakened heart, and dominance of the brow chakra. They can go to college and all that; but they, too, cannot hold relationships. Because of excessive intellectualism, they too become vulnerable to political manipulations and join the tent of socialism and meritocracy

In this way, both groups—lower educated and higher educated are socially shortchanged and politically manipulated. This is the reason that the political and social polarization is killing democracy.

Higher education—quantum style—elucidated in the previous chapters will empower those who are ready. The challenge of quantum style lower education is to institute the changes necessary to empower our youngsters irrespective of the tent their parents live. This will reduce, if not eliminate the lower education higher education chasm.

Can Youngsters be Taught Subtle Concepts of Consciousness, Experiences, and Quantum Physics?

People often ask me (Amit), have you tried teaching quantum physics and consciousness to grade school students? I have to admit that a few times I have tried to teach quantum physics to anyone below high school level, I hadn't had much success.

But there is another way. To create an ambience for youngsters from which they can learn to be curious about their experiences, even their consciousness. Witness the follow story from the Upanishads:

A young boy named Satyakama (significantly, a Sanskrit word meaning desirer of truth) comes to renowned teacher Gautama. Gautama appreciates his dedication to truth (he was straightforward in admitting that he was the son of a prostitute), but of course there is the dilemma—the kid has not gotten any basic education like the other kids in his class. He has to be taught privately, but where is time? Gautama thinks for a while and appoints the kid to look after his cows, take them to the pasture for feeding etc. If Satyakama is intelligent he can learn from nature; so thought the guru.

Satyakama started attending to the cows. He is curious: why did the teacher send me to keep company with cows? Could they be teachers?

One day he began imagining. He asked a cow of his imagination, *"How do I know reality?"*

The cow answered (in his imagination of course), *"Look around you. What do you see?*

"I see the bright Sun and how it lights up all the four directions I look."

Suddenly, an intuition comes to the kid. Consciousness is Reality, like the Sun, the only source of light that removes ignorance. It comes from four directions—the four kinds of experiences we have—sensing, feeling thinking, and intuiting.

Another day, another sitting with imagination. He asks his imaginary cow, *"How do I learn about the purpose of sensing?"* Once again, the answer comes intuitively, *"Look at the solid earth for advice."*

He asked the earth in his imagination. *"What can you teach me about reality?*

"I represent the solid, rigid, unchanging stuff where Reality can be manifestly represented—solid matter can make memory of all the other experiences."

That is interesting. *"But how do I know about these other experiences, like feeling?"* He asks his imaginary cow and the cow says, *"Ask the swan."*

Satyakama imagines a swan and after a while the swan tells him via an intuition, *"Feelings are flexible and moving like the water that I swim in. Just as water makes you wait, feelings can linger in you for a while"*

"Now I want to know about thinking, but who will teach me that?" When he asks the cow, the cow sends him to an eagle this time. So Satyakama imagines an eagle and asks, *"What in nature represents thinking?"* The intuition comes, *"Thinking is always moving, like the air in which I fly. Unless you mix it with feelings and make emotional thought, it does not linger."*

And then Satyakama wants to know about intuition. For that he is asked to look at lightnings. He meditates and the intuition comes, Lightnings are sudden. But when they come, they can clear away all the old growth of an entire forest, clearing and making room for the new. The objects of intuitions—the archetypes—are transformative.

He goes back to his imaginary wise cow and says, *"I have followed your instructions and now know this about reality: Reality is consciousness. It comes to us in the form of four experiences; these experiences and analogous to the four elements of nature—earth, water, air, and fire. Is this all that is to reality?"*

The boy patiently waits for an answer. In a while, the intuition comes. *"The four experiences represent the potentialities of Reality of that which can be experienced as objects. This much is right. But who experiences these objects? Who is the knower?"*

The boy engages in further dialogs with his imaginary wise cow. After a time, the intuition comes to him: Reality is consciousness. Then it must be consciousness that is experiencing the objects of experience.

But when he tries to find the experiencer in himself, he is disappointed. As soon as he attempts to look for his "I"—the experiencer in him, it becomes his me, an object.

He asks his wise cow. This time the cow is silent, no more intuitions. Desperate, he goes back to Gautama. *"Reverend sir. How do I find the experiencer—manifest consciousness, the I—within me?"*

Gautama replies. *"You have to undertake the hero's journey. I will initiate you."*

In Hinduism, this story is the basis for all initiation ceremonies which Brahmins—the truth seekers—have to engage that is like a second birth. The initiation into the exploration of meaning and purpose.

Today, with quantum science in our hands, we can do better. We can teach the youngster some quantum science before undertaking the initiation into hero's journey.

Meaning and Purpose

The author Patrick Rothfuss made an important observation in his book *The Name of the Wind*:

When we are children we seldom think of the future. This innocence leaves us free to enjoy ourselves as few adults can. The day we fret about the future is the day we leave our childhood behind. At about age of 15, development psychology tells us, this awareness of the future falls on us like a ton of bricks in the form of the questions of meaning and purpose (see chapter 4). It is a necessary preparation for adulthood.

But we have to remember this. Our carefree childhood does not entirely have to miss questions of meaning and purpose. Old cultures knew this; they taught young children fairy tales to teach them about purposive values. And young adults were taught some mythology. These practices aught to be revived.

Finally, as the Upanishadic story indicates, nature around a kid has a lot to teach him or her. Early education must facilitate this.

The Current Challenges of Lower Education

A very big challenge now faces us: how to make changes to lower education so that children may participate in quantum higher education later when they have that option. Right now, child development between age 0-5—where parents do the job of education and often not even parents but childcare professionals—is a very murky area of developmental psychology.

There is also reincarnational inheritance, how much is triggered and when, depends on the circumstances. Each child's case is different.

Girls and boys also have the male-female difference. But the socio-cultural tendency traditionally has been to neglect the emotional development of boys by encouraging them to exacerbate the brain's tendency of emotion suppression via not attending to feelings in the body. Boys' feelings remain somewhat foreign to them. This makes them socially superficial oriented around outer activities. Currently, some cultures are, an example is USA, promoting emotion suppression even for little girls with disastrous consequences later because of the resulting deficiency of their relationship capabilities.

However, as discussed before, in all cultures, parents traditionally encourage girls' positive feelings in the heart, love, and urge them to be other love oriented. Whereas boys, already awkward in relationship due to their brain structure, are encouraged in developing self-reliance, strong navel chakra, a side effect of which is self-indulgence and narcissism if no awakening of the navel takes place.

With a little help from the parents, many children may be quite capable of giving even some mental form to intuitions starting about age 3 contributing to their moral development. Today, parents in rich countries more and more start formal pre-school mental education instead around age 3 virtually eliminating this possibility.

Archetypal Dichotomies

Archetypal dichotomies of the collective unconscious affect everyone irrespective of their age. Social institutions such as racism exacerbates these dichotomies.

Of these dichotomies, at least one, the beauty-ugly, can best be worked on when we are small children. Small children can easily be taught about the inner beauty of all people; after that it is only a question of familiarity. If the society is not segregated, this is easy. Otherwise not.

Pre-operational stage: Living-nonliving and Life-death dichotomies, Reincarnational Issues

Children become curious about the difference between living things and nonliving things. This is a tricky subject to explain without using sophisticated concepts of quantum science. But here is an excellent opportunity for parents to teach their children about the difference between sensory and extra-sensory communication in our relationship with plants and trees. Ask children to feel the vitality of an indoor living plant and compare it with the experience of an artificial plant.

Children become very curious about life versus death issue if one of their close relatives, a grandparent for example, passes. If the child is more than three years old, here is a parent's grand opportunity to talk about complex issues of not only death but also survival after death and reincarnation.

If a child is born with a personal archetype (dharma), then the child's educational interests are tied up with its dharma. Good parenting demands the use of multiple modalities of expression making room for all the different archetypes to express—drawing, singing, dancing, poetry, math, science, money, sports, relationships (with both other children and adults).

Not having its interest perked is a contributing factor to a child's autism, especially if the child lacks mirror neurons, a brain hardware defect that produces deficiency of social skills.

On top of all these worldview—and culture—imposed difficulties there is no scope for organized parental education now-a-days, not for children aged 0-5.

Then there is Piaget's theory. Piaget almost entirely based his theories and observations on mental cognition and ego development, for example stages of pre-operational, concrete operational and formal operational structures of thought. They are quite appropriate for children's mental operational development—con-op and form-op, but not very useful when you add all the new contexts of pre-operational child development, as well as teen development of sexuality. See chapter7.

Piaget did recognize the importance of creativity in child development. According to Piaget, a child learns by accumulation and adaptation followed by assimilation that involves reflective abstraction, a process similar to do-be-do-be-do followed by insight as the creative process. But Piaget missed the contribution of reincarnation, a concept not permitted in his materialist/organismic worldview. Reincarnation messes up the neat chronology of the stages of development. Taking this uncertainty of when reincarnational karma will be triggered points to the importance of the multiple channels of development besides intellectual. Personality theory a la quantum science shows personalities come as head type (intellectuals measurable by IQ), body type (practical and street smart, not measurable by IQ), and heart type (emotional, not measurable by IQ). For the non-intellectuals, current educational systems based on Piaget's theory and the like is not of much use. This is likely a major contributing factor toward the lower-educated higher-educated divide.

Even for intellectual development, the reincarnational contribution of the *gunas* makes a huge contribution. Obviously, one size cannot fit all. One rate of intellectual development does not suit kids of different *guna*-balance.

CONCRETE AND FORMAL GRADE SCHOOL EDUCATION, AGE 6-11, 11-18

Here the issues are a bit simpler, though challenging ones, nevertheless.

Take one of the very first issues. To change the emphasis from primacy of matter to primacy of Consciousness. In a previous age, educators had to do a total purging of religious concepts from liberal education to satisfy the demands of secularism. The current task is equally challenging; the emphasis is to bring an integrative attitude: both matter and spirit are important. One for the hardware; the other for the software and the interface.

Children of this age have to learn their ways of relating to the world, part time on their own: they need to develop their ego and ego's repertoire. The current situation emphasizes the 3 R's. This is good. However, this must not be exclusive. Creativity demands the participation of the quantum self. And education of children from age 6-11 requires creativity as well.

Otherwise, children develop tamas, staying at the base level of human condition and do rote learning and at best logical learning to develop IQ intelligence. But no appreciation for meaning in that; for that they need understanding—inner creativity that helps to develop their individuality as well.

We have to supplement the 3 R training with the three I's:

1. Inspiration: this to inject Consciousness and quantum self (expanded Consciousness) and archetypes, feelings

(to make room for curiosity and passion), and inclusivity (education is not an individual thing anymore; the reason I am in a school with others is not only, so I learn social skills but also, I learn cooperatively, not competitively.

2. Imagination: the logical learning of the 3 R's contracts consciousness when we process with thinking. Imagination without bounds of strict logic liberates us. This combined with creative intentionality creates an opening for the next I.

3. Intuition. This facility is almost forgotten now. It is essential to bring it back to lift young people from ignorance to wisdom eventually.

For all this, teacher training is very important. Teachers who walk their talk, who are transformed with quantum higher education, are needed.

Worldview and Teaching Moral Development

In an earlier time when the religious worldview dictated children's education, morality was taught as a bunch of do's and don'ts, imposed authoritatively, by parents, by teachers, by religious preachers. These teachings became part of a person's memory bank, the superego in their personal unconscious in Freudian terms. It certainly affected behavior but not the inner being except raising unresolved conflicts.

In the current materialist schema for public school education, education is entirely about the outer, and is behaviorally oriented. In other words, it is behavioral change and communication skills, political correctness for example in behavior and communication, that is sought when looking at moral development, not inner transformation of the ego, not any expansion of Consciousness. Those are not part of the materialist worldview.

The difference between the older approach and the newer is important to notice. The education was behavioral in both approaches. However, the religious approach invariably raised conflicts between what Freud called Id, the suppressed-repressed part of the personal unconscious and the moral teachings of the superego. In the materialist approach, the conflict is eliminated.

Good or bad? From a transformative point of view, the materialist approach produces a callousness, superficiality, about moral issues that continues to the adult age with disastrous consequences.

Read Dostoyevsky's incisive novel *Brothers Karamazov*; the brothers spend hour arguing moral issues, to resolve their inner conflicts. So did I (Amit) when I was growing up in 1940's India. Do middle school children still do that? Hardly.

Currently, children get indoctrinated in the materialist dogma pretty early, even six-year-olds get the message: everything is made of elementary particles, those little building blocks of matter. Suppose it is made clear even at the elementary school level, that only matter (and physical energy) is made of elementary particles, not *everything* in our experience. Then introduce the idea: Consciousness is primary. Elucidate: Just as from looking at matter in the bulk that we experience, the elementary particle picture can be understood only as an abstraction, similarly, our experience of Consciousness at the ego/me leaves it obscure that Consciousness at the ground level is a state that include all things and all experiences. But we can conceptualize it only as an abstraction. This is what the religions try to do with simplified confusing dualist concepts. And now quantum science has caught up with the game of how to avoid dualism, and the current quantum models of abstraction have been experimentally verified to a high degree.

Can we really teach all this? My personal experience is that even eighth graders can handle this much abstract concept. The important thing at the age 6-11 level is to teach the students techniques of meditation practices that expand their experiential arena; there is no better proof of expansion of consciousness, the inclusive ability of consciousness, than that.

The other important abstraction is the conceptualization of physical versus nonphysical experiences; that is, to explain why and how we draw the distinction between our experience of matter visa a vis the experience of thinking and feeling. Recently, psychological research has revealed that children naturally distinguish between mind and matter as dualities. Materialists have to work hard to change that experiential knowledge into accepting material monism. The quantum educator's task is relatively simple. Monistic idealism is easier to comprehend for children because of their familiarity with the quantum self and expansion of consciousness.

The challenge here is to do introduce the idea of consciousness splitting into dualities and explain the difference of this from dualism. Parents and teachers have to keep on teaching that all experiences come from Consciousness; they are all aspects of Consciousness, that Consciousness is not only the subjects (either in the contracted state of the ego or the expanded state of the quantum self) but also the objects.

Eventually, by the time the kids reach age 11, they should have the full range of human experiences: sensing, feeling, thinking, and intuitive thoughts and positive emotions, so that they can grasp the conceptual abstraction to the idea of the experience of intuition.

The highest degree of abstraction, the concept of archetypes, may now be introduced. When ethics and morality are conceptually introduced based on the archetypes of goodness, love, justice, and truth, it makes all the difference.

Simultaneously, if we continue to veer education towards eliminating the fundamental dichotomies as much as possible, especially inner and outer, and the students learn what it is to be ethical inside when one is partaking in ethical behavior outside, that, too, makes a huge difference.

Sociologists speak of moral development in terms of personal, ethnocentric, and world-centric, but without expanded Consciousness to include the other, first in intimate relationship, then in one's own ethnic group, then in humanity at large, what does it mean to be moral? Bridging inner-outer dichotomy is essential here.

It would still be a puzzle to the eighth grader why we experience the world as outer as well as inner, why the dichotomy in the first place, that explanation cannot be introduced short of high school. Only in high school science can we attempt to teach the student the concept of possibility wave.

There are other aspects of inner-outer integration that can be introduced in the middle school. Emphasize cleanliness of mind when we teach cleanliness of the child's desk or room at home. First, they are taught the awareness of the outer inner dichotomy; now they train for balancing them.

In the same way, age 6-11, is excellent time to begin the education about the importance of dreams as a purely internal experience. Talking about dreams in connection with Australian aborigines perks the interest of eighth graders.

6-11 is also the prefect age for introducing kids to lifelong practice of meditation and yoga, and the like.

It is time to abolish all female-male segregation, racial segregation, segregation based on sexual preference or transgender at all educational institutions all over the world. With the paradigm shift to quantum and the social re-enchantment of values, this should come soon.

Free Will

The biggest detriment to moral development throughout history is the ambiguity about free will. Do we have free will or do we not? Under the religious worldview, the idea that it is all God's will, created moral ambiguity. If we keep God pleased, we can indulge in immoral behavior. And of course, without free will to act, how can I be responsible for my actions?

With materialist science to guide you, it is worse. You are machine; you don't have free will. Moral development is a social convenience. The penal system is an anachronism (how can we punish criminals when their atrocious actions are merely mechanical?) but necessary for maintaining social order. Ultimately, the materialist scientists justify everything based on survival needs.

In quantum science, free will exists. Students can easily be taught the ability of saying "no" to conditioned tendencies and teachers can explain this ability as free will to suspend the old making room for the new.

Teen Education: High School

One of the supreme life-challenge of the teen age is sexuality (the other is meaning and purpose). Under the religious worldview, sex was only an animal thing, for procreation. Therefore, abstention was morally prescribed until marriage, and even after marriage sex was to be used only for procreation. Materialist worldview has liberated sex from moral restriction, but sex education is barely better than the previous age of parents talking to children entering puberty about "the birds and the bees." Teenagers now get a graphic education about the mechanics of sex, sexual anatomy at least.

Materialist science has nothing to say about the relationship aspect of sex except about the pleasure bond, the neuroscience of sex, the sex hormones, again, the mechanical side of sex.

Sex for pleasure without the understanding of relationship leads to objectification of the sexual partner which is fine in the materialist philosophy since there is nothing but objects but of course has been disastrous for women, who talk about the heart, who want love. Furthermore, the objectification leads to sexual abuse in high school campuses.

Materialists don't like to talk about meaning because meaning is not computable. Materialists have also missed the question of purpose entirely because all actions are causal following the seventeenth century idea of Newton about how matter changes movement.

Consciousness-based science changes all that. Modern post-materialist psychology in the form of transpersonal psychology has introduced relationship between I and you making we; however, the "we" is implicitly conceived as local. The reason is the lack of taking the feeling and emotional dimension of the human being into account. When we do that, and when we also take purposive action initiated by archetypal intuition into account, the relationship aspect of sex can be properly treated.

The basic idea of course is that the organ functions are purposive, and they evolve with human development. In human beings, from the get-go, the purpose of the sexual organs is not just procreation, not even procreation plus pleasure, but is also for the exploration of love.

In this way, sex education can now be much better and close a major gap in the education of teenagers.

In general, quantum education in high school is not only about thinking and concept-development but also about living—a balanced approach of thinking and feeling including the archetypes to an extent.

The Transition from Lower to Higher Education: Who Should Pay for Higher Education?

Of course, high school is also the time when education terminates for many for a variety of reasons and those trends will continue in human societies for a long time yet.

Internet technology and the high cost of greed-driven materialist higher education prevalent today, is rapidly leading us to a necessary fundamental change. The technocrat education and higher education for the rest of the student body must bifurcate in two branches. In-campus proximity education with emphasis on hardware, science, and math, engineering, and technology will continue. For this branch, software learning will become information oriented of necessity—time constraint. And here, the subject really does get sophisticated from year to year, either in math or in laboratory practice. Therefore, the current model of 4-year undergraduate education and another 5-10 years of post-graduate education cannot be avoided. The education will be expensive, and the government must pitch in to a degree to help, providing low-interest loans for example.

The higher education in Health-care (except training for surgery), psychology and mental health, economics, business and other social sciences required to achieve personal and social prosperity, the arts and humanities will move to almost all Internet, up to the master's level at least. Some proximity will be necessary for experiential and transformational aspect of quantum higher education. This is a huge saving.

Another saving will come in this way. There is no increasing sophistication in any of these nontechnical fields. Much of the sophistication you see now is bureaucratic due to legalities necessary in origin to make the job more complicated than it needs to be. Law education is a perfect example, but other fields have the same tendency. There is of course a lot to learn. The subjects overlap; even theoretical ideas and concepts of physics have to part of the curriculum. But it is our view that we can easily complete all necessary conceptual and transformational education in no more than 2 years for bachelor's and two years for Masters; and all this being mostly on the Internet will enable students to have even full-time jobs and still complete the education.

The cost of education can no longer go up exponentially since government bureaucracy and student loans are not involved. Students take the responsibility for their own higher education.

And teachers! They have to be transformed of necessity; greed is eliminated. Motivated people will not go into the teaching profession with the purpose of money making. Their objective is satisfaction with the service they render, with the relationships they make, with the lives they help transform.

For practicing professionally with archetypal exploration in any field will require intense transformational changes and will require some proximity education. And perhaps getting a PhD will require at least 3 years, may be more.

Politics of Irony

First realize this. There is once again a big way that technology has shifted people's mindset. This is the ubiquitous use of information technology—men, women, rich, poor. Information processing makes us into computers; it severs all our connection to Consciousness, Oneness. In the absence of that connection, because of the lack of the experience of expanded Consciousness, we become confused about who are, what is the meaning and purpose of human life, etc.

The situation is not totally hopeless; the laws of the movement of Consciousness ensured via the phenomenon of reincarnation that there would always be people, call them old souls, who have been into soul-making for a while. Right now, there are about 15% of the entire humanity that belongs to this category.

This then is how that 85%-15% divide took place. Can 15% of people help the vast zombie-like majority to wake up to their humanity? There are a few reasons to be hopeful.

And there is irony here. Look at the political scene in most countries. The worldview is polarized between materialist science and religion. Materialist science is pseudoscience—science with dogma. And so is religion pseudo-spirituality—spirituality with dogma. The science group is locked into an incomplete but rational system of thought to guide itself, an incompleteness that really hurts is that archetypes are denied any scientific validity. The religious group is stuck with a belief system that they know cannot stand up to the standards of rationality of the science group, so they defy even scientific data in favor of literal interpretation of their scriptures. And doing that they, too, undermine the archetypes.

One irony is this. The materialist science group denigrates all archetypes including truth. This gives the religious group to make their own "science" using their belief system. If truth is not absolute, how can you choose between the two? So, the science group more and more gives up reliance on theory. Surely, nobody can object to data, fact. But it is not that simple; without theory to guide us, we are driven by our prejudices; materialists themselves denounce very reliable data from parapsychology and consciousness research.

The irony continues. One can make science into pure empiricism, but one cannot impose empirical data on a society which denies the concept of truth. Especially, when the empirical efforts needed to collect the data is so complex that they are not easy to verify. This makes it easy to produce "data" that contradicts the "scientific" data. This is what is happening today in the developed countries. There is data proving global warming; there is data proving that it may not be so. There is data proving that wearing masks prevent CVD-19 infection; there is data proving masks may not be effective.

More irony. The elite of the materialist science group, being rational realizes that the archetypal values are necessary to have civilized systems to a run a society. So, they invent a new philosophy called humanism (by the way, Karl Marx did virtually the same thing) that restores the values. But living them means transformation! So, they hope since people are about behavior, if they impose "politically correct" value-oriented behavior, that will suffice to make a civilized society. The rest can be done by imposing laws.

But of course, the elites of the religious group sees through the hypocrisy; they have been preaching those values in similar ways for millennia! Except that they were not big experts on sophistry in the olden days. They simply maintained they are exempt from ethics because they are already perfected beings; sins do not affect them.

Add the information technology. Both groups create their own information network and make sure their adherents get only the set that conforms to their belief system. The two groups have different sets of truth. How can they ever communicate? Believe it or not, this is the socio-political polarization we have created.

How do you feel about all this from the point of view of a real open dogma-free scientific paradigm such as quantum science? You know that the case for materialist science is half-truth. And you sympathize with the frustration of this group with the religious group denying the fact of data! Of course, you also know all too well, that the same materialist group is denying the validity of other liberating data in order to hold on to their particular dogma. The saving Grace is this saying: old paradigmers never change but they do die. The younger generations are the cause for some hope. But even for that group, there is the addiction to information processing to hinder progress.

The religious group does not have any respect for science right now. When science becomes dogma free via the effort of the next generation of scientists, the story may change. Without reaction, action cannot get anything to engage. When scientists are no longer keen on destroying religion, the antipathy of religion toward science will give way. Sooner or later, religions will find their way back to their spiritual origin.

The Way Out

You have to understand the problem of education for human development right now in the context elucidated above. Why does the religious group not see the validity of the data on global warming? Why does the religious group deny health professionals and their data in the current coronavirus crisis? These questions that materialists ask, are the same questions that frustrate the new paradigm researcher, why don't the materialists accept the quantum data on nonlocality, on distant viewing, on vital energy?

The answer is simple. We cannot do without the archetypes. We cannot develop civilization further. And yet, you cannot convince people with dogma. For millennia, people are fighting about these issues. You cannot resolve them easily without going to the route cause. Curing symptoms does not do the job.

It is the limitations of collective unconscious that our ancestors created: the archetypal dichotomies—good and evil; beauty and ugly; truth and lie that is also causing the current crisis. We have to integrate these dichotomies within ourselves and then spread the integration software we so develop.

We have to build on what we have. We have the built-in capacity for sympathy. We also have some capacity for love: the built-in universal software of romantic love, the personal software that everyone gets to build on the experiences of mother's love. Goodness and love go to the basics of balancing the good-evil dichotomy. If we can balance the negative emotional circuits of violence, domination, hatred, and the like with positive emotional software via the exploration of goodness and love, that goes a long way toward regaining some emotional intelligence. Then the journey of other archetypal exploration such as that of truth, justice, and beauty becomes feasible.

Furthermore, having some software for goodness and love helps one to collectivize the self-centered approach people generally take in the pursuit of abundance and power.

This part is quite doable for the 15%. This is an achievable goal of transformational education formulated here.

The difficult problem is how to spread this software to the 85%. Somehow, we not only have to transform but transform collectively using nonlocal Consciousness. If you liked this book, if you are inspired to undertake the hero's journey and contribute to the return of the archetypes in our lives and professions, if you are persuaded to develop community consciousness as you transform, there is hope.

Further reading: For ideas on collective evolution/development, read Goswami, *Quantum Biology and the Ascent of Humanity*. For personal transformation, read, Goswami, *The Quantum Activism Handbook*; Goswami, Blake, and Stewart, *Quantum Activation*; Goswami and Pattani, *The Quantum Science of Happiness*; and the book *Quantum Spirituality* by Onisor and Goswami, and the upcoming *The Awakening of Intelligence*.

EPILOGUE

The Story of Quantum Activism Vishwalayam—an Institution of Quantum Transformational Education

We hope a substantial number of you, dear reader, are wondering about if there is an institution of Transformational quantum higher education already in place where you can receive such higher education of hero's journey that we are propounding?

The two of us and friends, some in America, some in Brazil, some in India, some in Europe, have founded such an institution. We call it Quantum Activism Vishwalayam. The Sanskrit word *Vishwa* means the world; *layam* means home. Vishwalayam stands for home of the world. It is the educational wing of the Center for Quantum Activism in the USA; it is also the center's liaison to the University of Technology, Jaipur, India, a fully government affiliated university. As the department of Quantum Science at UOT we are now offering a Masters and PhD program in Quantum Science of Health Prosperity, and Happiness, bonafide quantum higher education **mostly taught online.**

Why use the word activism? Because as we believe that students educated the quantum way will become activisms of a new breed, activists who transforms the world as they transform, they not only change but they share with humanity the agency and eventually the fruits of their change.

We won't tell you more about what we teach; this book gives enough of a preamble. But we will use this space to tell you about the trials and tribulations needed to manifest this institution. It is good illustration of how the quantum science of manifestation works!

Yes, it began with an inspiration. In 1973, I (Amit) was at the height of my academic physics career. I was invited to a physical society meeting; I gave the talk but when the next speaker spoke;

I thought he did a better job, and I was jealous. This went on the whole day, speaker after speaker presented, and I was jealous of all of them. Even in the evening at a party, I was jealous of the other men because they were attracting more female attention. The jealousy energy gave me a raging heartburn. At about 1 am in the morning, I found that I had exhausted my entire packet of antacids. I became disgusted and I went outside on to the fresh ocean air. Suddenly, unexpectedly, came this thought, "Why do I live this way?" and with that came the conviction that I can do otherwise; I can do happy physics. I can go more congruence between the way I think, the way I live, and the way I do physics. That intention followed the inspiration immediately. But no intuition.

A year later, I dreamt my father. My father was a spiritual guru of sorts. When I was growing up as a little child, I often wondered what do the five or six disciples who gathered around him on a mat do actually. And yet I was aware that my father had a being that had a calming effect on people including myself. In the dream, my father had a snake in his hand; he threw it at me, and I caught it.

Wow! I was intrigued, what does the dream mean? A friend explained. My father is a symbol of transformation for me. A snake signifies change. I need to look at spiritual transformation. That resonated with me, and I started hobnobbing with meditating groups, Muktananda followers in town, Zen priori, New Age meditation groups, that sort of thing.

One thing led to another. I went to a workshop and the leader taught us what he said was the latest quantum wisdom: We create our own reality. Can we create a car that way? Somebody asked. Of course, we can, the leader said. "But look! That takes a lot of meditative intention difficult to manifest in a five-day workshop. So, I want you to practice manifesting a parking space for your care."

That was a daunting task, I found out. I drove to the downtown where the workshop was half hour early; did my intention just as he taught us and drove around looking for a spot. I ran out of time and ended up paying for my parking. And the same experience replayed every following day! I could not do it! The only consolation was that only a few succeeded.

But the exercise perked my curiosity about the message that quantum physics is supposedly giving. I have practiced quantum physics since my college days; never heard of that one. A little research showed it was a slogan created by the physicist Fred Alan Wolf.

Ok, that's how came the intuition of what I needed to look at: quantum physics and the ideas of the power of Consciousness it hints at, ideas that were laden with paradoxes and controversies at the time.

When finally, I solved the paradoxes and discovered the quantum physics of Consciousness that I shared with you in the book. Then I came across a fellow who had an organization with a great name: World Peace University. And that was it! An idea but no substance. I easily convinced him. Why don't we teach the science of Consciousness that quantum physics is helping us create? Surely, such teaching will also teach people peace! He agreed along with another bunch of New Agers who were trying to develop a spiritual farming community.

This did not fly. Reluctantly, I had to admit to myself that you cannot make people commit to a science that is in the making; that takes much more risk that a student can be expected to take. Of course, that never stopped people with money and organization. All over America, educational institutions were springing up teaching what can at best be called post-materialist education. A hodgepodge of different ideas that more concentrated on pointing out the defects of the existing worldviews that give the students a coherent substitute. These institutions still exist and generally speaking, they do a good job in creating some sort of vehicle for people to ride, for people who are searching for meaning and purpose but cannot find in the existing establishment institutions. The good thing students learn is some of the age-old techniques of transformation like meditation. The bad thing that their thinking ends up being very confused between all the models of Consciousness they are taught. As I said, this is good for researchers, not for students who are looking to a new way to live and earn livelihood.

This situation still prevails. The post-materialists cannot agree with each other's model of Consciousness! How can they? They neither follow the old spiritual way which is to spend years and years in the transformational journey without knowing exactly what you are supposed to be doing; or the way of exploring the possibility of a modern dogma-free science with a conjunction of theory and experiment.

For me, it was a long waiting game during which I explored and found such a science in quantum physics integrating the message of the wisdom traditions. The long exploration time was good for me because I was forced to make progress in both ways of wisdom: the experiential and the scientific. In 2009, I was fairly certain that something needs to be done to attract the attention of the post-materialists to look at the wonderful new results quantum science was giving: a science of Consciousness and experience; an integration of all the different transpersonal and unconscious-based theories of psychology with materialist approaches; an integration of the modern and traditional ways of healthcare; a new theory of evolution that integrated Darwin's ideas with Consciousness-based ideas of Teilhard de Chardin and Sri Aurobindo; even a science of reincarnation. The post-materialists were too attached to their easy systems approach and the philosophy of holism; they still are at the time of this writing. I started a new movement: quantum activism. It did not change the minds of many of the post materialists, but it did touch a chord with people aspiring for meaning, especially women.

I started the movement of quantum activism and established the Center for quantum activism. It developed quite a bit of interest in America, Europe, and India, and especially in Brazil.

In 2016, I was invited to present my ideas about the quantum science of Consciousness at a spiritual organization in Pyramid Valley, Bangalore. My talk created a stir. Afterwards, I was discussing my work with the guru of the organization and some of the important decision makers. At some point I expressed some bitterness about the obvious: people who dare to look at the new quantum science paradigm seriously cannot be found much anywhere. The physicists who "know" physics were afraid of delving into Consciousness; people who try to "know" Consciousness were afraid of delving into physics. The guru said, "Why don't you start your own university?" Simultaneously, the businessman who funded the ashram was nodding his head in approval and very soon everybody in the room were enthusiastic with the idea.

I was dumbfounded. Was the intention formed in the nineteen eighties coming to fruition? Well, it was still too early; politics entered, politics entered, and things broke down.

Months later, it was my friend Anil Sinha who I met at the Pyramid Valley, came to the rescue with the help of a spiritual businessman named Dinesh Kukreja in Jaipur. By that time, I had acquired a few more co-founders, especially Valentina, the co-author of this book. Dinesh helped us with the finances for running a pilot program. The program did not succeed in terms of getting a whole bunch of committed students. But the few who attended did find quantum education transformational.

After the pilot program, Dinesh withdrew his financial support because of personal problems, so I had to face a big decision. Up till then, all my life, I have been a researcher and a teacher but neither a businessman nor a leader.

Several years earlier, I wrote a book *Quantum Economics* in which I proposed an extension of Capitalism to catch up with the quantum worldview. This book talked about how a quantum leader must also be an entrepreneur in subtle businesses, businesses that use vital energies, mental meaning, and transformational archetypes as business commodities. I realized this was the time to walk my talk. The result is: Quantum activism Vishwalayam offering Masters and Ph. D. as a school of Quantum science of Health, Prosperity, and Happiness at the fully government affiliated university,the University of Technology in Jaipur, India.

This was a long journey, and so is its intended fruit—for people who are ready, education toward the transformation and the exploration of the higher needs of life that makes human life worth living. Fortunately, when your objective is consonant with the purposive movement of Consciousness, it ends in success. Mine did and so will yours.

Are you ready to make a commitment to make thinking, living, and livelihood congruent? For the Masters it is a two-year commitment and for PhD the commitment is longer: three and a half to six years. Email us at info@amitgoswami.org.

BIBLIOGRAPHY

Aspect, A.; Dalibard, J.; and Roger, G. 1982. "Experimental test of Bell inequalities using time-varying analyzers." *Physical Review Letters,* vol, 49, p. 1804.

Aurobindo, S. (1996). *The Life Divine.* Pondicherry, India: Sri Aurobindo Ashram.

Beauregard, M. (2012). *The Spiritual Brain.* N.Y.: Harper

Bloom A, (1987). *The closing of the American mind.* N.Y.: Simon and Schuster.

Briggs, J. (1990). *Fire in the Crucible.* L.A.: Tarcher/Penguin.

Byrd, R. C. (1988). "Positive therapeutic effects of intercessor prayer in a coronary care unit population." *Southern Medical Journal,* vol. 81, pp. 826-29.

Cairns, J (1993). *Science.* Vol 260, Issue 5112. pp. 1221-1222; Cairns, J. (1988). *Nature* 335: p. 142

Campbell, J. (1949) *Hero with a Thousand Faces.* N.Y.: Pantheon books

Campbell, J. (1990) *Hero's Journey.*

Chardin T P (2015), *The phenomenon of Man:* The great library collection: Toronto, Canada.

David, B. (1980), Wholeness and implicate order: Routledge London and NY

Dr. Seuss. (2012) *The Lorax*: Illumination entertainment

Erikson E H (2014), The Stages of Psychosocial Development: GRIN Verlag

Gilligan C, (1982). *In a different voice*: London: Harvard University Press

Goleman, D. and Davidson, R. (2012) *Altered Traits.* N.Y.: Avery

Goswami, A. (1993). *The Self-Aware Universe: How Consciousness Creates the Material World.* N.Y.: Tarcher/Putnam.

Goswami, A. (1994). *Science within Consciousness: a monograph.* Petaluma, CA: Institute of Noetic Sciences.

Goswami, A. (2000). *The Visionary Window: A Quantum Physicist's Guide to Enlightenment*. Wheaton, IL: Quest Books.

Goswami, A. (2001). *Physics of the Soul*. Charlottesville, VA: Hampton Roads.

Goswami, A. (2004). *The Quantum Doctor*. Charlottesville, VA: Hampton Roads.

Goswami, A. (2008). *God is not Dead*. Charlottesville, VA: Hampton Roads.

Goswami, A. (2008). *Creative Evolution*. Wheaton, IL: Theosophical Publishing House.

Goswami, A. (2014). *Quantum Creativity: Think Quantum, Be Creative*. N. Y.: Hay House.

Goswami, A. (2009) The Quantum Activism Handbook

Goswami, A. (2019) and Onisor, R. V. (2019. *Quantum Spirituality*. Delhi, India: Blue Rose.

Goswami, A. and Onisor, R. V. (2021). *The Quantum Brain*. Delhi, India: Blue Rose.

Goswami, A. Blake, C. and Stewart, G. (2021) *Quantum Activation*.

Goswami, A. and Pattani, S. (2022). *The Quantum Science of Happiness*. Eugene, OR: Luminaire Press

Goswami, A. *Quantum Biology and the Ascent of Humanity*. To be published.

Goswami, A. and Onison, V. R. *The Awakening of Intelligence*. To be published.

Gould SJ. (1977). *Paleobiology*, Vol. 3, No. 2. (Spring, 1977), pp. 115-151.

Grinberg-Zylberbaum, J. Delaflor, M., Attie, L., and Goswami, A. (1994). "Einstein-Podolsky-Rosen paradox in the human brain: the transferred potential." *Physics Essays*, vol. 7, pp. 422-28

Grof, S. (1997). *The Cosmic Game*. N.Y.: SUNI Press.

Harary, Y. (2015). *Sapiens: a Brief History of Humankind*. London: Harvill Secker.

Hawking, D. (1994). *Power Vs. Force*. N.Y.: Hay House

Hume, D. *Causality*. Internet encyclopedia of philosophy

Jung, C. J. (1971). *The Portable Jung*. J. Campbell, ed. N. Y.: Penguin.

Jung, C. J. (1969). *The Archetypes of the Collective Unconscious*. Princeton, NJ: Princeton University Press.

Lashley, K. S. (1950), 'In search of the engram', Symposium of the Society for Experimental Biology, 4, 454–83.

Laszlo, E. (2021). *My Journey*. N.Y.: Select Books.

Maslow, Abraham. (1971). *The further reaches of human nature*, NY: Penguin/Arkana

Merrell-Wolff, F (1994). *Philosophy of Experience*. Albuny, NY: SUNY Press

Newberg, A. (2009) *How God changes your brain*.

Penrose, R. (1991). *The Emperor's New Mind*. N.Y.: Penguin.

Pert, C. (1997). *Molecules of Emotion*. N.Y.: Scribner.

Piaget J, Inhelder B, (2000). *The psychology of the child* N. Y.: Basic Books

Radin, D. (2009). *The Noetic Universe*. London: Transworld Publishers.

Riso, D. R. (1987). *Personality Types: Using the Enneagram for Self-discovery*. N.Y.: HarperCollins.

Searle, J. (1994). *The Rediscovery of the Mind*. Cambridge, MA: MIT Press.

Searle, J. 1980. "Minds, brains, and programs." *Behavioral and Brain Science. Vol. 3*, pp. 417-24.

Sheldrake, R. (1981). *A New Science of Life*. L.A.: Tarcher.

Shimony A, (1993) *The search for a naturalistic worldview* Cambridge: Cambridge University Press.

Teilhard de Chardin, P. (1961). *The Phenomenon of Man*. N.Y.: Harper & Row.

von Neumann, John. (1955). *The Mathematical Foundations of Quantum Mechanics*. Princeton: Princeton University Press.

INDEX

A

abundance 12, 15, 23, 42, 51, 52, 58, 65, 72, 73, 91, 105, 164, 169, 189, 192,
194, 196, 197, 198, 205, 245
Abundance 49
ambiguity 11, 39, 69, 86, 87, 238
Ananda 19, 155
Anterior 34
apara vidya 45
archetypal journey 113, 131, 132, 136, 139, 213
Archetype 169
attitudinal 50, 64, 73
Aurobindo 21, 109, 165, 191, 250, 253

B

Bhagavad Gita 204
biology 16, 50, 58, 61, 63, 71, 92, 95, 103
bonafide 247
Brahman 2
Brain 36, 38, 39, 76, 159, 174, 226, 253, 254, 255, 261, 264
breathing 31, 177
British 27, 147
Buddha 21, 66, 116, 207, 216

C

Capitalism 194, 195, 251
capitalist 17
Chakras 70
charisma 17, 59, 169, 170, 190, 222
Christianity 20, 78, 132, 207, 263
Civilization 46, 86
civilizations 49, 66
codification 42
Collapse 126, 127
Colonization 27
Columbia University 16
consciousness 2, 3, 18, 24, 26, 31, 32, 33, 34, 35, 37, 38, 39, 43, 45, 48, 50, 52,
60, 61, 67, 73, 77, 87, 91, 93, 94, 95, 96, 100, 103, 104, 105, 106, 123,
125, 126, 142, 179, 180, 181, 193, 204, 213, 216, 228, 229, 230, 235, 237,
243, 245, 261, 263

AMIT GOSWAMI, PHD, is a retired professor from the physics department of the University of Oregon (1968 to 1997). He is a renowned pioneer of the new paradigm of quantum science based on the primacy of consciousness.

In 2009, Amit started a movement called Quantum Activism, now gaining ground in North and South America, Europe, and India. At the same time, he has also established the Center for Quantum Activism (CQA) with headquarters in USA.

In 2019, he and his collaborators established an educational wing of CQA called Quantum Activism Vishwalayam (Home of the World), acting as Department of Quantum Science at the University of Technology in Jaipur, India, and developed a Master and PhD program in Quantum Science of Health, Prosperity and Happiness, an international program of transformative education.

Goswami has written several groundbreaking popular books based on research on quantum science and consciousness, amongst them, *The Quantum Brain, Quantum Spirituality and The Reenchantment of the Reality You Live,* (with Valentina R. Onisor, MD), *Quantum Psychology and the Science of Happiness* (with Sunita Pattani, MS), *The Self-Aware Universe, The Quantum Doctor, Physics of the Soul, Quantum Creativity and The Everything Answer Book.*

Amit was featured in the movie *What the bleep do we know?* and the documentaries *The Dalai Lama Renaissance* and *The Quantum Activist.*

Amit is a spiritual practitioner and calls himself a quantum activist in search of Wholeness.

VALENTINA R. ONISOR, MD, is a practicing physician, a pioneer of quantum integrative medicine specializing in family medicine. She integrates alternative medicine with various systems of complementary medicine (acupuncture, ayurveda, naturopathy, homeopathy and aromatherapy) into her practice.

Committed to consciousness awakening related sciences for over two decades, Valentina is also a yoga and meditation teacher (Sivananda Vedanta Forest Academy; Yoga Alliance; Universal Consciousness Ambassador, CSETI). She has developed together with Amit Goswami, PhD, the transformative practice of Quantum Yoga, that integrates quantum science with traditional spiritual practices (Qigong, Yoga, meditation, esoteric Christianity, Tibetan tradition).

As a leader in transformational education, Valentina serves as a Director of Educational Programs at Center for Quantum Activism, USA, and is a faculty, at Department of Quantum Science, UOT, Jaipur, India. She is also the co-founder of Quantum Activism Vishwalayam, India. She is a lecturer at Quantum Academy in Brazil, and at Fundación Icloby in Spain. Additionally, Valentina is currently offering a number of courses and workshops oriented towards healing and spiritual transformation all over the world. Her work has been featured in various interviews and radio shows.

She is co-author of (along with Amit Goswami, PhD) *Quantum Spirituality, The Quantum Brain, The Reenchantment of the Reality You Live,* and *The Quantum Integrative Medicine,* as well as of the upcoming books, *The Return of the Archetypes, The Awakening of Intelligence,* and *The Quantum Science of Love and Relationships.*